Dear Ann,

Thank you for your very kind & generous support of our efforts to protect land & water for people & nature.

Tiffany
C. McKenna

The Quotable Nature Lover

The Quotable
Nature Lover

COMPILED BY
JOHN A. MURRAY

A NATURE CONSERVANCY BOOK

THE LYONS PRESS

For A. F.

First edition, 1999

Printed in the United States of America

Design and composition by Compset, Inc.

10 9 8 7 6 5 4 3 2

Library of Congress Cataloging-in-Publication Data
The quotable nature lover / compiled by John A. Murray.
        p.   cm.
    Includes index.
    ISBN 1-55821-942-0
    1. Nature Quotations, maxims, etc. I. Murray, John A., 1954–
PN6084.N2Q68 1999
508—dc21

THE NATURE CONSERVANCY

The mission of Nature Conservancy is to preserve plants, animals, and natural communities that represent the diversity of life on Earth by protecting the lands and waters they need to survive.

The Nature Conservancy operates the largest private system of nature sanctuaries in the world—1,340 preserves in the United States alone. All of them safeguard imperiled species of plants and animals. The Conservancy also works internationally, helping like-minded partners protect land in Latin America, the Caribbean, Asia, and the Pacific.

Come visit.
Walk quietly.
Listen carefully.

You'll see and marvel at the astounding diversity of life.

Contents

Introduction

Nature and books belong to the eyes that see them.
—Ralph Waldo Emerson, "EXPERIENCE"

In December of 1998 an arctic front drifted south from Alaska and the Yukon into the continental United States. Everywhere it went there were frozen pipes and broken furnaces, ice, fog and snowdrifts, downed phone lines and power cables, dead batteries and flattened tires, influenza and frostbite, traffic accidents and airport delays. The lynx loved it, of course, as did the ravens, who were finding plenty to eat. The bison, covered with rime, were not in the least disturbed. The trout merely settled deeper into their slumbers. In nearly every large town, the cold fatally embraced at least one person—a cross-country traveler marooned on a lonely stretch of road, an elder who had wandered away from the nursing home, a teenage skier who had somehow gotten lost in the woods. When the cold finally reached Denver, where I live, it decided to stay for a while. The visit, like that of certain relatives, seemed interminable. In the end, it lasted about two weeks.

This state of affairs proved fortuitous, though, in that I was compelled to retire, bearlike, to the depths of my solstice den, and work, with a captive singularity of purpose, on this book. Each day, and sometimes well into each frosty night, I focused my energies on providing readers with the best quotations I could for each of these ten subjects: Place, Solitude, Exploration, Nature's Fury, Beauty, Liberation, Seasons, Mystery, Community, Stewardship. At any one time there were perhaps a hundred books piled in stacks around my computer table. At times I literally disappeared from the world.

In my search for a consistent philosophy of life I have been continuously inspired and guided by nature. This has been true from the earliest period of my recollection. Over the last forty-four years nature has provided me peace in the midst of turmoil, an alternative

form of companionship in seasons of solitude, invigo-
ration when fatigued, and understanding when faced
with some riddle, paradox, or injustice. In this, I have
experienced nothing new. The Greek and Roman Stoics
made a close relationship to nature the basis of their
belief system two thousand years ago, as did, more
recently, such philosophers as Jean-Jacques Rousseau
and Henry David Thoreau. I have always believed that
nature provides the "way" to enlightenment, to freedom from that which encumbers us, to a deeper understanding of the human condition, and to a fuller capacity for creativity, happiness, and love.

Since 1995, when I donated the royalties of my
book *The Great Bear* to the Conservancy's Pine Butte
Preserve in Montana, I have been actively committed
to the organization. To me, The Nature Conservancy
represents the best in the world of conservation—
people working at the community level to preserve
nature for future generations. This book is built
around the generous spirit at the core of the Conser-

vancy's philosophy—the belief that dedicated people working together can help protect our natural world.

I hope that readers find as much pleasure in refamiliarizing themselves with the accumulated wisdom of the past on these subjects as I have. It is a book that I, and perhaps you, have always wanted to include in the library, and now we both have it. Many apt quotations have eluded me, no doubt, and can be added in future editions. Feel free to send your favorites to me at P.O. Box 102345, Denver, CO 80250.

JOHN MURRAY

Place

Once in his life a man ought to concentrate his mind upon the remembered earth, I believe. He ought to give himself up to a particular landscape in his experience, to look at it from as many angles as he can, to wonder about it, to dwell upon it.

—N. SCOTT MOMADAY, *THE MAN MADE OF WORDS*

The lovely places. The lonely places. The lost and forgotten places. The places where we go to turn our backs on the world, the places where we go to try to get back into the world. The places where we fell in love, or out of love, or came to an understanding, or made a decision, and the places where we stood alone with some truth about ourselves, our kind, our world. The crowded places. The secret places. The places where history was made. The places that will never be again. The places that may still be made whole again. The places that seem untouched by time. The places that seem to have been touched a little bit too much by time.

One thinks, in meditating upon such a list, most wistfully of the lost places, of those wonderful landscapes that somehow, through ignorance or accident or against all best efforts, slipped away from us. Of the Upper Missouri River country that George Catlin painted with such skill, that will never be seen again: its vast bison herds and endless prairie. Or of the canyon of the Tuolumne River—John Muir's beloved Hetch Hetchy—

that was filled with High Sierra snowmelt in order to provide water for the Bay Area. It was, judging from surviving photographs, as lovely as Yosemite Valley. Or of John Wesley Powell's wild Glen Canyon, with all its fabled arches, glens, alcoves, spring-fed gardens, cliff dwellings, and hidden side canyons. It was, Edward Abbey wrote, "the living heart of the Colorado Plateau," and now it is the second largest reservoir in the world.

One thinks, too, of those places that *were* saved and how close we came, in many cases, to losing them forever. The Nature Conservancy calls some of these spectacular places the Last Great Places, from New York's Adirondack Mountains to the Florida Keys to the Tallgrass Prairie of the Great Plains to the Colorado Plateau. Internationally, they range from Belize's Maya Mountains and Bolivia's Noel Kempff Mercado National Park to Micronesia's Palau Islands and Indonesia's Komodo National Park. We must all work to keep such magnificent places sacred, special, and protected for generations to come.

For each home ground we need new maps, living maps, stories and poems, photographs and paintings, essays and songs. We need to know where we are, so that we may dwell in our place with a full heart.

—Scott Russell Sanders, "Buckeye"

In that country which lies around the headwaters of the Gila River [in southwestern New Mexico] I was reared. This range was our fatherland; among these mountains our wigwams were hidden; the scattered valleys contained our fields; the boundless prairies, stretching away on every side, were our pastures; the rocky caverns were our burying places. As a babe I rolled on the dirt floor of my father's teepee, hung in my tsoch at my mother's back, or suspended from the bough of a tree. I was warmed by the sun, rocked by the winds, and sheltered by the trees as other Indian babes.

—Geronimo, *Autobiography*

A landscape that is incomparable, a time that is gone forever, and the human spirit, which endures.

—N. SCOTT MOMADAY, *THE WAY TO RAINY MOUNTAIN*

———

I can see the farm [on which I grew up] still, with perfect clearness . . . can call back the solemn twilight and mystery of the deep woods, the earthy smells, the faint odors of the wild flowers, the sheen of rain-washed foliage, the rattling clatter of drops when the wind shook the trees, the far-off hammering of woodpeckers and the muffled drumming of wood pheasants in the remoteness of the forest, the snapshot glimpses of disturbed wild creatures scurrying through the grass . . . I can call back the prairie, and the loneliness and peace, and a hawk hanging motionless in the sky, with his wings spread wide and the blue of the vault showing through the fringe of his end feathers.

—MARK TWAIN, *AUTOBIOGRAPHY*

Nature was here something savage and awful, though beautiful . . . Here was no man's garden, but the un-handselled globe. It was not lawn, nor pasture, nor mead, nor woodland, nor lea, nor arable, nor waste land. It was the fresh and natural surface of the planet Earth, as it was made forever and ever . . . It was Matter, vast, terrific . . . the home, this, of Necessity and Fate. There was clearly felt the presence of a force not bound to be kind to man . . . We walked over it with a certain awe.

—HENRY DAVID THOREAU, "KTAADN"

In calling up images of the past, I find that the plains of Patagonia frequently cross before my eyes; yet these plains are pronounced by all wretched and useless. They can be described only by negative characters; without habitations, without water, without trees, without mountains, they support merely a few dwarf plants. When then, and the case is not peculiar to myself, have these arid wastes taken so firm a hold on my memory? Why have not the still more level, the greener and more fertile Pampas, which are serviceable to mankind, produced an equal impression? I can scarcely analyze these feelings, but it must be partly owing to the free scope given to the imagination.

—CHARLES DARWIN, *THE VOYAGE OF THE* BEAGLE

The edge of the sea is a strange and beautiful place. All through the long history of Earth it has been an area of unrest where waves have broken heavily against the land, where the tides have pressed forward over the continents, receded, and then returned. For no two successive days is the shore line precisely the same.

—RACHEL CARSON, *THE EDGE OF THE SEA*

Being aware of the splendor of the seasons, of the natural world, makes us understand man's critical need for wild places. Living with familiar things and moving in the seasons can fulfill that profound need common to us all: a sense of place.

—JO NORTHROP, *COUNTRY MATTERS*

A sense of place, to me, is being in touch with the natural world, finding health and balance and renewal in nature and the seasons. If we are in a place that we love, where we are comfortable, where we have invested ourselves, so much the better.

—JO NORTHROP, *COUNTRY MATTERS*

It is often true that the best things we do in some strange way take place within us long before we come to the ground itself. The physical domain of the country had its counterpart in me. The trails I made led outward into the hills and swamps, but they led inward also.

—JOHN HAINES, *THE STARS, THE SNOW, THE FIRE*

The geography of my life wrinkles with water, with rivers, and with fish. Always there has been water: dark seas and bright rivers, blue oceans and mountain streams hissing down deep canyons of layered dark stones that are time's boneyards.

—HARRY MIDDLETON, *THE BRIGHT COUNTRY*

I grow into these mountains like a moss. I am bewitched. The blinding snow peaks and the clarion air, the sound of earth and heaven in the silence, the requiem birds, the mythic beasts, the flags, great horns, and old carved stones, the rough-hewn Tartars in their braids and homespun boots, the silver ice in the black river, the Kang, the Crystal Mountain.

—PETER MATTHIESSEN, *THE SNOW LEOPARD*

As time went by, I realized that the particular place I'd chosen was less important than the fact that I'd chosen a place and focused my life around it. Although the island has taken on great significance for me, it's no more inherently beautiful or meaningful than any other place on earth. What makes a place special is the way it buries itself inside the heart, not whether it's flat or rugged, rich or austere, wet or arid, gentle or harsh, warm or cold, wild or tame. Every place, like every person, is elevated by the love and respect shown toward it, and by the way in which its bounty is received.

—RICHARD NELSON, *THE ISLAND WITHIN*

Three months of camp life on Lake Tahoe would restore an Egyptian mummy to his pristine vigor, and give him an appetite like an alligator. The air up there in the clouds is very pure and fine, bracing and delicious. And why shouldn't it be?—it is the same the angels breathe.

—MARK TWAIN, *ROUGHING IT*

You need not be intelligent to love a place. Love of place is a natural emotion. It comes free to us all.

—CAROL BLY, "IN THE MATERNITY WING, MADISON, MINNESOTA"

My prayer is that Alaska will not lose the heart-nourishing friendliness of her youth—that her people will always care for one another . . . and that her great wild places will remain great, and wild and free . . . That is the great gift Alaska can give to the harassed world.

—MARGARET MURIE, *TWO IN THE FAR NORTH*

To the lover of wildness, Alaska is one of the most wonderful countries in the world.

—JOHN MUIR, *TRAVELS IN ALASKA*

———

Home is the place where, when you have to go there,
They have to take you in.

—ROBERT FROST, "THE DEATH OF THE HIRED MAN"

———

The eye could follow the river winding and see where
canyons notched the blue mountains. One peak looked
like an ear turned on its side. Trees and river and the
wide valley and the brown hills on either side floated in
the fall haze, lazy and comfortable and sleepy now with
autumn. It was as pretty a place as a man could wish, a
prime place except that the world seemed dying and a
man's hankering was cold and foolish in him.

—A. B. GUTHRIE JR., *THE BIG SKY*

I had a farm in Africa, at the foot of the Ngong Hills. The Equator runs across these highlands, a hundred miles to the North, and the farm lay at an altitude of over six thousand feet. In the day-time you felt that you had got high up, near to the sun, but the early mornings and evenings were limpid and restful, and the nights were cold. The geographical position and the height of the land combined to create a landscape that had not its like in all the world.

—ISAK DINESEN, *OUT OF AFRICA*

I like exploring. I like not knowing when and where I'll end up. That way I get easily diverted and find the new, the unexpected. To learn to know something is less to gaze upon it from known paths and vistas than to walk around it and see it obliquely.

—BERND HEINRICH, *THE TREES IN MY FOREST*

Some places are like some poems; we return to them again and again, and each time they reveal new meanings and new delights ... Such a place is the Great Smoky Mountains National Park, a unique remnant of primeval America, fifty-four miles long and twenty wide. Like a rock in midstream, they stood virtually untouched by the main current of westward migration. The course of empire took its way through easier channels, and thus a bit of the original forest survived—the finest woods, I believe, east of the Mississippi and the best hardwood stands you will find anywhere.

—PAUL BROOKS, *ROADLESS AREA*

After supper, we would spread out our sleeping bags in a circle, heads pointing to the center like a covey of quail, and watch the Great Basin sky fill with stars. Our attachment to the land was our attachment to each other.

—TERRY TEMPEST WILLIAMS,
REFUGE: AN UNNATURAL HISTORY OF FAMILY AND PLACE

When I go back, as I must, to live in a world almost wholly man-made and almost wholly absorbed in problems which man himself has created, I shall often return in memory to things seen and done during my desert interlude . . . I shall not forget its lesson: much can be lacking in the middle of plenty; on the other hand, where some things are scarce, others, no less desirable may abound.

—JOSEPH WOOD KRUTCH, *THE DESERT YEAR*

Into my heart an air that kills
  From yon far country blows:
What are those blue remembered hills,
  What spires, what farms are those?

—A. E. HOUSMAN, "INTO MY HEART AN AIR THAT KILLS"

Here, on our native soil, we breathe once more.

—WILLIAM WORDSWORTH, "SONNET COMPOSED NEAR DOVER"

I remember that the Gabilan Mountains to the east of the valley were light gay mountains full of sun and loveliness and a kind of invitation, so that you wanted to climb into their warm foothills almost as you want to climb into the lap of a beloved mother.

—JOHN STEINBECK, *EAST OF EDEN*

Anyone who has traveled in the wilds knows how much he looks forward to the time of day when he can lay down his burden and make camp. He pictures the ideal place and all that he must find there . . . As shadows begin to lengthen, the matter of a campsite takes precedence over everything else, as it has for ages past whenever men have been on the move. The camp with its fire has always been the goal, a place worth striving for and, once attained, worth defending against all comers.

—SIGURD F. OLSON, "CAMPFIRES"

I shall not be there. I shall rise and pass.
Bury my heart at Wounded Knee.

—STEPHEN VINCENT BENÉT, "AMERICAN NAMES"

My daughter is quiet beside me in the front seat, until at last she sighs and says, with a child's poetic logic, "This reminds me of the place I always like to think about."

—BARBARA KINGSOLVER, "THE MEMORY PLACE"

We are old friends—the White Mountains [of New Hampshire] and I.

—WILLIAM O. DOUGLAS, *My Wilderness*

I do not understand how anyone can live without some small place of enchantment to turn to.

—MARJORIE KINNAN RAWLINGS, *Cross Creek*

My deepest longing is to live in a world that respects life in every form, a world whose people have a fierce love and loyalty to the earth, and their particular place thereon.

—LORRAINE ANDERSON, *SISTERS OF THE EARTH*

That we were poor made no difference in that beautiful place. The flowers bloomed for us as thickly as for others, the breeze came in at evening and cleaned the heated atmosphere. We could run out into those woods and know that hope is everlasting.

—DOROTHY ALLISON, "PROMISES"

There is a dreaminess here where creation continues to happen all around us in time that is alive.

—LINDA HOGAN, "CREATION"

Solitude

I feel it wholesome to be alone the greater part of time. To be in company, even with the best, is soon wearisome and dissipating. I love to be alone. I never found the companion who was so companionable as solitude.

—Henry David Thoreau, *Walden*

Every so often a disappearance is in order. A vanishing. A checking out. An indeterminate period of unavailability. Each person, each sane person, maintains a refuge, or series of refuges, for this purpose. A place, or places, where they can, figuratively if not literally, suspend their membership in the human race. For some the sanctuary is a weekend farm in upstate New York, far from the steel and concrete canyons of the city. Hundreds of acres of forest and meadowland in every direction. A wooden dock and canoe down by the lake. A belted kingfisher flying by. For others it is a sun-washed beach on the south Atlantic coast. Driftwood and seashells. Dolphins playing in the surf. Tall white clouds building over the purple sea. I had a friend once who raised a cabin in the North Cascades, where the snowdrifts last through summer's longest day. He spent a fortnight there every August. In that way he was able to endure the other fifty weeks below. Another friend departs regularly for the slickrock canyons of southern Utah. We don't hear from him for a week. When he returns he is sunburned and able to sleep again.

Even presidents have had them. Jefferson re-treated to his mountaintop at Monticello, and Washington enjoyed solitary horseback rides. Lincoln was fond of long country walks. Teddy Roosevelt sought refuge in the vastness of the Dakota badlands. Later in life he ranged farther—the savannas of East Africa, the headwaters of the Amazon. Eisenhower came out to the Rockies every summer to fish by himself on the Fraser River. Kennedy preferred the privacy of a sail-boat, the only place in the world where he could get away from the clamor for a while. Ronald Reagan found solace on his ranch north of Los Angeles, an overgrown tract of live oaks and manzanita, coyotes and black-tailed deer.

Great minds have accomplished great things in solitude. Consider the paintings of Winslow Homer, or Georgia O'Keeffe, or Andrew Wyeth. Or the poems of Wordsworth, or the novels of Solzhenitsyn. Or the symphonies of Beethoven, once deafness had separated him from the world, or the songs of the old blues masters, when they were left alone by circumstance with their six-string guitars.

In the end our moments of solitude lead us back, refreshed and refocused, to society. In this process we may take our lessons from nature—from the stars, which sometimes gather together in bright groups and other times stand alone and apart; or the rivers, which pass many a quiet mile alone before joining in companionship with other streams; or the bears, which live in isolation much of the year, but join together for a time each summer as the salmon run.

Here was not field, nor camp, nor ruinous cabin, nor hacked trees, nor down-trodden flowers, to disenchant the Godful solitude.

—JOHN MUIR, "EXPLORATION IN THE GREAT TUOLUMNE CANYON"

At Saturday noon, on November third, a few days before the last general election, I rowed a small skiff into the current of the Colorado River, near the town of Moab, Utah, and disappeared for ten days. By choice. Since I lacked the power to make a somewhat disagreeable world of public events disappear, I chose to disappear from that world myself . . . I preferred this kind of solitude not out of selfishness but out of generosity; in my sullen mood I was doing my fellow humans (such as they are) a favor by going away.

—EDWARD ABBEY, *RIVER SOLITAIRE: A DAYBOOK*

Nothing can bring you peace but yourself.

—RALPH WALDO EMERSON, *ESSAYS*

The best remedy for those who are afraid, lonely or un-happy is to go outside, somewhere where they can be quiet, alone with the heavens, nature and God.

—ANNE FRANK, *THE DIARY OF A YOUNG GIRL*

O Solitude! if I must with thee dwell,
Let it not be among the jumbled heap
Of murky buildings: climb with me the steep,—
Nature's observatory; . . .

—JOHN KEATS, "SONNET: O SOLITUDE"

In all the earth there is no place dedicated to solitude.

—CHIEF SEATTLE, HEAD OF THE SUQUAMISH AND DUWAMISH
TRIBES, IN AN 1854 SPEECH

I will arise and go now, and go to Innisfree,
And a small cabin build there, of clay and wattles made:
Nine bean-rows will I have there, a hive for the honey-bee,
And live alone in the bee-loud glade.

—WILLIAM BUTLER YEATS, "THE LAKE ISLE OF INNISFREE"

I've known rivers:
I've known rivers ancient as the world and older than
   the flow of human blood in the veins.
My soul has grown deep like the rivers.

—LANGSTON HUGHES, "THE NEGRO SPEAKS OF RIVERS"

In solitude especially do we begin to appreciate the advantage of living with someone who knows how to think.

—JEAN-JACQUES ROUSSEAU, *CONFESSIONS*

Solitude is as needful to the imagination as society is wholesome for the character.

—JAMES RUSSELL LOWELL, *ESSAYS*

What was I capable of that I didn't know yet? What about my limits? Could I truly enjoy my own company for an entire year? Was I equal to everything this wild land could throw at me? I had seen its moods in late spring, summer and early fall, but what about winter? Would I love the isolation then with its bone-stabbing cold, its brooding ghostly silence, its forced confinement? At age 51 I intended to find out.

—RICHARD PROENNEKE, ON SETTING OUT TO SPEND ONE YEAR ALONE IN THE ALASKAN WILDERNESS (FROM *ONE MAN'S WILDERNESS*)

Wilderness . . . The word suggests the past and the un-known, the womb of earth from which we all emerged. It means something lost and something still present, something remote and at the same time intimate, something buried in our blood and nerves, something beyond us and without limit.

—EDWARD ABBEY, DESERT SOLITAIRE

I turned with growing concentration to Nature as a sanctuary and a realm of boundless adventure; the fewer people in it, the better. Wilderness became a dream of privacy, safety, control, and freedom. Its essence is captured for me by its Latin name, *solitudo.*

—EDWARD O. WILSON, NATURALIST

The wise employ their Solitude in pious counsels.

—SAINT PATRICK, A PARABLE OF PILGRIMS

If from society we learn to live,
'Tis solitude should teach us how to die:
It hath no flatterers.

—LORD BYRON, "CHILDE HAROLD'S PILGRIMAGE"

Many times during the season, I have in my solitude a
visit from the bald eagle. . . . I have little doubt that
what attracted me to this spot attracts him,—the seclu-
sion, the savageness, the elemental grandeur.

—JOHN BURROUGHS, "WILD LIFE ABOUT MY CABIN"

A man can be himself alone so long as he is alone; . . . if
he does not love solitude, he will not love freedom; for it
is only when he is alone that he is really free.

—ARTHUR SCHOPENHAUER, *THE WORLD AS WILL AND IDEA*

For many years I was self-appointed inspector of snow-storms and rain-storms, and did my duty faithfully, though I never received one cent for it.

—HENRY DAVID THOREAU, *JOURNALS*

It is not good to be too much alone, even as it is unwise to be always with a crowd.

—HENRY BESTON, *THE OUTERMOST HOUSE*

When I went to be alone at Djemila [in the deserts of northern Algeria], there was wind and sun and a heavy, unbroken silence—something like a perfectly balanced pair of scales. And I would stand there, absorbed, confronted with stones and silence.

—ALBERT CAMUS, *THE WIND AT DJEMILA*

We are rarely proud when we are alone.

—Voltaire, *Philosophical Dictionary*

———•••———

I feel so independent now. I can go or be anywhere I want to. I have the few essentials I need, and the few others things I need or want I can derive from the land.

—David Cooper, on starting his 200-mile solo trek through the Brooks Range (from *Brooks Range Passage*)

———•••———

Oh, let me lie where a mother's prayer
And a sister's tear might mingle there,
Where my friends can come and weep o'er me,
Oh, bury me not on the lone prairie.

—Traditional Western song
("Bury Me Not on the Lone Prairie")

I have been one acquainted with the night.

—ROBERT FROST, "ACQUAINTED WITH THE NIGHT"

I feel so lonesome
You can hear me when I moan
I feel so lonesome
You can hear me when I moan.

—ROBERT JOHNSON, "TERRAPLANE BLUES"

Then he talked from ten till long after midnight, the steady, rambling monologue of an old man who has lived alone too long.

—ROBERT MARSHALL, DESCRIBING AN OLD BACHELOR LIVING ALONE IN THE ALASKAN BUSH IN *ALASKAN WILDERNESS*

He did not remember when he had first started to talk
aloud when he was by himself.

—ERNEST HEMINGWAY, *THE OLD MAN AND THE SEA*

Away, away from men and towns,
To the wild wood and the downs,—
To the silent wilderness,
Where the soul need not repress
Its music.

—PERCY BYSSHE SHELLEY, "TO JANE, THE INVITATION"

To have passed through life and never experienced solitude is to never have known oneself. To have never
known oneself is to have never known anyone.

—JOSEPH WOOD KRUTCH, *THE DESERT YEAR*

Out in the world you may, very occasionally, look down at night from a high and lonely vantage point onto the swarming life of a great city and catch a frightening glimpse of your own personal insignificance. But that is not quite the same thing [as being alone in the Grand Canyon]. You do not feel, achingly, the utter insignificance of all mankind, and you therefore escape the sense of final, absolute, overwhelming helplessness.

—COLIN FLETCHER, *THE MAN WHO WALKED THROUGH TIME*

Our real journey in life is interior.

—THOMAS MERTON, CIRCULAR LETTER TO FRIENDS, SEPTEMBER 1968

In those old times, the young men used to go off alone in the hills and fast for four nights. This was called the wu wun, starving. They had no shelter and no covering. If he fasted to the end, after four days, the old man went to him and brought him down to the camp . . . Not everyone starved and to only a part of those who starved did the vision come.

—George Bird Grinnel, describing the Cheyenne vision quest ritual in his narrative of the 1874 Custer Black Hill expedition

The river was an awful solitude, then.

—Mark Twain, *Life on the Mississippi*

Turning southward, they paddled down the stream, through a solitude unrelieved by the faintest trace of man.

—Francis Parkman, *Pioneers of France in the New World*

Thus let me live, unseen, unknown;
    Thus unlamented let me die;
Steal from the world, and not a stone
    Tell where I lie.

—ALEXANDER POPE, "ODE ON SOLITUDE"

[I am] grateful, that by nature's quietness
And solitary musings, all my heart
Is softened, and made worthy to indulge
Love, and the thoughts that yearn for human kind.

—SAMUEL TAYLOR COLERIDGE, "FEARS IN SOLITUDE"

Solitude is a thing we crave.

—RICK BASS, THE BOOK OF YAAK

She came to the desert after seeing her gaunt face in the mirror, the pallor that comes when everything is going out and nothing is coming in.

—TERRY TEMPEST WILLIAMS, *COYOTE'S CANYON*

I would like to learn, or remember, how to live. I come to Hollins Pond not so much to learn how to live as, frankly, to forget about it . . . I think it would be well, and proper, and obedient, and pure, to grasp your one necessity and not let it go, to dangle from it limp wherever it takes you.

—ANNIE DILLARD, *TEACHING A STONE TO TALK*

[Wilderness] can be a means of reassuring ourselves of our sanity as creatures, a part of the geography of hope.

—WALLACE STEGNER, *THE SOUND OF MOUNTAIN WATER*

Exploration

Walking, I am listening to a deeper way. Suddenly all my ancestors are behond me. Be still, they say. Watch and listen. You are the result of the love of thousands.

—LINDA HOGAN, "WALKING"

It begins early, the desire to explore. It is probably encrypted in our natures, rooted in our beings, implanted in the strands of DNA that so powerfully determine who we are and what we do.

Some of us are more compelled to explore than others. One thinks of the Phoenicians, who always had to see what was over the horizon. Or of the Vikings, who found and settled the New World hundreds of years before Columbus was a visitor to the Spanish court. Such names as Boone and Crockett, Bridger and Carson come to mind. A hundred other figures rise up from the pages of history—John Coulter and his incredible report (which no one believed) on the wonders of the Yellowstone country, Major John Wesley Powell and his unlikely rafting trip through the Grand Canyon, Sir Edmund Hillary and his "impossible" ascent of Mount Everest. Each was impelled to probe the limits, both within and without. Each changed forever how we view the world, and ourselves, for if one person has stood on the summit of the tallest mountain, or uncovered the workings of the sun's great engines, or found a way to paint the aftermath of Guérnica, so, in a sense, has the entire human race.

When I think of my own generation on this subject of exploration I consider many things. I recall first that in the year I was born—1954—whole provinces of Africa and Antarctica remained unmapped by air, the genetic code had yet to be deciphered, and space travel was the stuff of comic books. By the time I was in third grade photographic satellites had overflown the entire Earth, James Watson had been awarded the Nobel Prize, and manned space launches were regularly viewed on television. From those early years I can still hear a young president exhorting the nation to explore "new frontiers of the mind." The rest, for my generation, has been the stuff of legend—manned landings on the Moon, interplanetary spacecraft roaming Mars, the Hubble telescope and Dantean views of distant galaxies.

As Edward O. Wilson writes in his book *Naturalist*, "When the century began, people still thought of the planet as infinite in its bounty. The highest mountains were still unclimbed, the ocean depths never visited, and vast wildernesses stretched across the equatorial continents. Now we have all but finished mapping the physical world, and we have taken the measure of our dwindling resources. Troubled by what we have wrought, we have begun to turn in our role from local conqueror to global steward."

In my heart I will be an explorer naturalist until I die.

—EDWARD O. WILSON, *NATURALIST*

Now, when I was a little chap, I had a passion for maps. I would look for hours . . . and lose myself in all the glories of exploration. At that time there were many blank spaces on the earth, and when I saw one that looked particularly inviting on a map I would put my finger on it and say, "When I grow up I will go there."

—JOSEPH CONRAD, *HEART OF DARKNESS*

The value [of exploration] to the individual is in the thrill of adventure and in the fact that exploration is perhaps the greatest aesthetic experience a human being can know.

—ROBERT MARSHALL, LETTER TO MELVILLE B. GROSVENOR, MARCH 1, 1935

Whenever I find myself growing grim about the mouth; whenever it is a damp drizzly November in my soul; whenever I find myself involuntarily pausing before coffin warehouses, and bringing up the rear of every funeral I meet; and especially whenever my hypos get such an upper hand of me, that it requires a strong moral principle to prevent me from deliberately stepping into the street, and methodically knocking people's hats off—then, I account it high time to get to sea as soon as I can. This is my substitute for pistol and ball. With a philosophical flourish Cato throws himself upon his sword; I quietly take to the ship. There is nothing surprising in this. If they but knew it, almost all men in their degree, some time or other, cherish very nearly the same feelings towards the sea with me.

—HERMAN MELVILLE, *MOBY-DICK*

Come, my friends,
Tis not too late to seek a newer world.
Push off, and sitting well in order smite
The sounding furrows; for my purpose holds
To sail beyond the sunset, and the baths
Of all the western stars, until I die.
It may be that the gulfs will wash us down;
It may be we shall touch the Happy Isles,
And see the great Achilles whom we
knew. Though much is taken, much abides; and though
We are not now that strength which in old days
Moved earth and heaven, that which we are, we are—
One equal temper of heroic hearts,
Made weak by time and fate, but strong in will
To strive, to seek, to find, and not to yield.

—ALFRED, LORD TENNYSON, "ULYSSES"

It is not down on any map, true places never are.

—HERMAN MELVILLE, *MOBY-DICK*

. . . do they call that exploring? Why they had everything they could ask for. They don't know anything about hardship. They ought to get out in the hills where they have to live on themselves, and can't radio for help every time they get in trouble.

—ERNIE JOHNSON, AS QUOTED BY BOB MARSHALL IN
ALASKA WILDERNESS

We have an unknown distance yet to run; an unknown river yet to explore. What falls there are, we know not; what rocks beset the channel, we know not; what walls rise over the river, we know not. Ah, well! We may conjecture many things.

—JOHN WESLEY POWELL,
EXPLORATIONS OF THE COLORADO RIVER AND ITS CANYONS

Be the Mungo Park, the Lewis and Clark and Frobisher to whole new continents within you, opening new channels, not of trade, but of thought. Every man is the lord of a realm beside which the earthly empire of the Czar is but a petty state, a hummock left by the ice . . . What was the meaning of that South Sea Exploring Expedition, with all its parade and expense, but an indirect recognition of the fact that there are continents and seas in the moral world, to which every man is an isthmus or an inlet, yet unexplored by him, but that it is easier to sail many thousand miles through cold and storm and cannibals, in a government ship, with five hundred men and boys to assist one, than it is to explore the private sea, the Atlantic and Pacific Ocean of one's being alone.

—HENRY DAVID THOREAU, *WALDEN*

Have faith and pursue an unknown end.

—FRANCIS BACON, AS WRITTEN IN ROBERT F. KENNEDY'S DAYBOOK

I do not doubt every traveler must remember the glowing sense of happiness from the simple consciousness of breathing in a foreign clime where the civilized man has seldom or never trod.

—CHARLES DARWIN, *THE BRAZILIAN FOREST*

The object of your mission is to explore the Missouri River, and such principal streams of it, as by its source and communication with the waters of the Columbia, Oregon, Colorado or any other river, may offer the most direct and practicable water communication across this continent for the purposes of commerce.

—THOMAS JEFFERSON, "INSTRUCTIONS TO CAPTAIN MERIWHETHER LEWIS," JUNE 20, 1803

Much have I traveled in the realms of gold,
And many goodly states and kingdoms seen;
Round many western islands have I been
Which bards in fealty to Apollo hold.
Oft of one wide expanse had I been told
That deep-browed Homer ruled as his
    demesne,
Yet did I never breathe its pure serene
Till I heard Chapman speak out loud and bold:
Then felt I like some watcher of the skies
When a new planet swims into his ken;
Or like stout Cortez when with eagle eyes
He stared at the Pacific, and all his men
Looked at each other with a wild surmise
Silent, upon a peak in Darien.

—JOHN KEATS, "ON FIRST LOOKING INTO CHAPMAN'S HOMER"

Out through the fields and the woods
And over the walls I have wended;
I have climbed the hills of view
And looked at the world, and descended;
I have come by the highway home,
And lo, it is ended.

. . .

Ah, when to the heart of man
Was it ever less than a treason
To go with the drift of things,
To yield with a grace to reason,
And bow and accept the end
Of a love or a season?

—ROBERT FROST, "RELUCTANCE"

I am one of those people who deeply resents not having been born in the 19th century when there were still open places to explore.

—BRUCE BABBITT, QUOTED IN *THE LOS ANGELES TIMES*, 1987

Two hours after midnight land appeared, at a distance of about two leagues from them. They took in all sail, remaining with the mainsail, waiting for day, a Friday on which they reached a small island. Immediately they saw naked people, and the admiral went ashore in the armed boat. When they had landed, they saw very green trees and much water and fruit of various kinds. The admiral took possession of the island for the King and Queen.

—CHRISTOPHER COLUMBUS, OCTOBER 12, 1492

The mightiest river in the world is the Amazon. It runs from west to east, from the sunset to the sunrise, from the Andes to the Atlantic . . . The gigantic equatorial river-basin is filled with an immense forest, the largest in the world . . . We were within the southern boundary of this great equatorial forest, on a river which was not merely unknown but unguessed at, no geographer having ever suspected its existence.

—THEODORE ROOSEVELT, DOWN AN UNKNOWN RIVER

The day has passed delightfully. Delight itself, however, is a weak term to express the feelings of a naturalist who, for the first time, has wandered by himself in a Brazilian forest . . . To a person fond of natural history, such a day as this brings with it a deeper pleasure than he can ever hope to experience again.

—CHARLES DARWIN, FEBRUARY 29, 1832, WHILE EXPLORING THE FORESTS OF COASTAL BRAZIL

I was led, at an early period of life, by commercial views, to the country North-West of Lake Superior, in North America, and being endowed by Nature with an inquisitive mind and enterprising spirit . . . I not only contemplated the practicability of penetrating across the continent of America, but was confident in the qualifications, as I was animated by the desire, to undertake the perilous enterprise.

—SIR ALEXANDER MACKENZIE, WHO ON JULY 22, 1793, BECAME THE FIRST PERSON TO CROSS NORTH AMERICA

Above us the sky took a blue so deep that none of us had ever gazed upon a midday sky like it before. It was a deep, rich lustrous, transparent blue, as dark as Prussian blue, but intensely blue.

—THE ARCHDEACON HUDSON STUCK, ON REACHING THE SUMMIT OF DENALI, JUNE 17, 1913

I will walk with leg muscles
which are strong
as the sinews of the shins of the little caribou calf.
I will walk with leg muscles
which are strong
as the sinews of the shins of the little hare.
I will take care not to go towards the dark.
I will go towards the day.

—WORDS TO BE SPOKEN WHEN SETTING OUT ON A LONG JOURNEY (IGULIK ESKIMO)

As we advanced the mountains became more and more precipitous until finally they culminated in the Gates of the Arctic. Fortunately this gorge was not in the continental United States, where its wild sublimity would almost certainly have been commercially exploited. We camped in the very center of the Gates, seventy-four miles from the closest human being and more than a thousand miles from the nearest automobile.

—ROBERT MARSHALL, FROM *ALASKA WILDERNESS: EXPLORING THE CENTRAL BROOKS RANGE*

That as no species of information is more ardently desired, or more generally useful, than that which improves the science of Geography; and as the vast Continent of Africa, notwithstanding the efforts of the Ancients, and the wishes of the Moderns, is still in a great measure unexplored, the Members of this club do form themselves into an Association for Promoting the Discovery of the Inland Parts of that Quarter of the World.

—SIR JOSEPH BANKS, ON FORMING THE AFRICAN ASSOCATION DURING A MEETING AT ST. ALBANS TAVERN IN LONDON, JUNE 9, 1788

It is always far to go when there are no friends at the end of the journey.

—AFRICAN PROVERB (BAVENDA TRIBE)

We saw, immediately below us, the Nile itself, strangely diminished in size, and now only a brook that had scarcely water to turn a mill. I could not satiate myself with the sight, revolving in my mind all those classical prophecies that had given the Nile up to perpetual obscurity and concealment . . . I stood in the spot that had baffled the genius, industry and inquiry of both ancients and moderns, for the course of near three thousand years . . . Though a mere private Briton, I triumphed here, in my own mind, over kings and their armies.

—JAMES BRUCE, ON DISCOVERING THE SOURCE OF THE NILE, 1770

I cut my initials on a tree, and the date 1855.

—DAVID LIVINGSTONE, ON BEING THE FIRST EUROPEAN TO VIEW VICTORIA FALLS

As life is action and passion, it is required of a man that he should share the passion and action of his time, at peril of being judged not to have lived.

—OLIVER WENDELL HOLMES, AS QUOTED BY ROBERT F. KENNEDY, 1966

Adventure is wonderful, but there is no doubt that one of its joys is its end.

—ROBERT MARSHALL, *ALASKA WILDERNESS*

Do not go where the path may lead, go instead where there is no path and leave a trail.

—RALPH WALDO EMERSON, *ESSAYS*

The voyage of discovery is not in seeking new land-scapes but in having new eyes.

—MARCEL PROUST, *REMEMBRANCE OF THINGS PAST*

The whole idea of travel is not to set foot on foreign land; it is at last to set foot in one's own country as a foreign land.

—G. K. CHESTERTON, *TREMENDOUS TRIFLES*

No pessimist ever discovered the secrets of the stars, or sailed to an uncharted land, or opened a new doorway for the human spirit.

—HELEN KELLER, *THE STORY OF MY LIFE*

Guided by my heritage of a love of beauty and a respect for strength—in search of my mother's garden, I found my own.

—ALICE WALKER, *IN SEARCH OF OUR MOTHERS' GARDENS*

Twenty years from now you will be more disappointed by the things you didn't do than by the ones you did do. So throw off the bowlines. Sail away from the safe harbor. Catch the trade winds in your sails. Explore. Dream. Discover.

—MARK TWAIN, *AUTOBIOGRAPHY*

Sit down before fact as a little child, be prepared to give up every preconceived notion, follow humbly wherever and whatever abysses nature leads, or you will learn nothing.

—THOMAS H. HUXLEY, *LAY SERMONS*

Behold the much-desired ocean! Behold! All ye men, who have shared such efforts, behold the country of which the sons of Comogre and other natives have told us such wonders!

—VASCO NÚÑEZ DE BALBOA, SEPTEMBER 25, 1513

And for me, the act of traveling, the act of encountering each new corner of the natural world, is bound to the idea of Advent. Advent is a season of preparation, of housecleaning, of getting ready for the miraculous. It's a season of joy-filled anticipation.

—W. SCOTT OLSEN, *AN ADVENT NATURE*

I spent three summers in Antarctica, in places beyond
    the horizon of most of my species.
The journeys all took place during that single long day
    that begins in October and ends
in March . . . We were scientists who had come to study
    [nature] . . . We were pilgrims in
the last new land on Earth.

—DAVID CAMPBELL, *THE CRYSTAL DESERT*

Dear Sir,

I am much pleased that you are going on a very long journey, which may by proper conduct restore your health and prolong your life.

Observe these rules:

1. Turn all care out of your head as soon as you mount the chaise.

2. Do not think about frugality: YOUR HEALTH IS WORTH MORE THAN IT CAN COST.

3. Do not continue any day's journey to fatigue.

4. Take now and then a day's rest.

5. Cast away all anxiety and keep your mind easy.

This last direction is the principal; with an unquiet mind neither exercise, nor diet, nor physic can be of much use.

I wish you, dear Sir, a prosperous journey, and a happy recovery, for I am

Dear Sir, Your most affectionate humble servant,
    Sam Johnson

—*THE SELECTED WORK OF SAMUEL JOHNSON*

Nature's Fury

"These bears, being so hard to die, rather intimidate us all."

—CAPTAIN MERIWETHER LEWIS, 1805

For every tranquil day at Edward Hopper's light-house on Cape Cod there is one filled with Winslow Homer's terrible shipwrecks. For every uneventful summer afternoon in the sunflower fields of western Kansas there is one in which tornadoes drop from the sky and flatten unsuspecting towns. For every family album photograph of Mount St. Helens still wrapped in old growth forest there is one in which it seems a nuclear bomb has just been detonated. One recalls the infamous April 1, 1946, tidal wave in the Aleutian Islands that swept an entire coast guard base out to sea, and five hours later drowned 159 people in Hawaii, and then went on to assault the coast of Chile; or the August 26, 1883, Krakatoa explosion that darkened skies on the other side of the Earth and cooled the northern hemisphere for several years (devastating, among other things, the cattle business of Charlie Russell's Montana); or the impact crater in the open desert near Winslow, Arizona, sizable enough to swallow the skyline of Manhattan, left apparently by a meteor.

No discussion of this subject would be complete without mention of those fine naturalists and explorers who have lost their lives as a direct result of nature's fury. Arctic America claimed more than its share of explorers, most notably Captain John Franklin, who disappeared in 1845 while searching for the Northwest Passage. The roster of those killed in Africa, which numbers in the dozens, begins with Mungo Park, who drowned in the Falls of Bussa on the Niger River. In more recent years there have been many other casualties around the world, including Aldo Leopold, who died while fighting a brush fire near his home, and my dear friend, the wildlife photographer Michio Hoshino, who was dragged from his tent and killed by a brown bear while on an expedition in the Russian Far East.

The most impressive example of nature's fury I have ever personally observed was ten years ago as I write these lines. I was on a flight from Denver, Colorado, en route to Fairbanks, Alaska. An hour after takeoff the plane passed over Jackson Lake in northwestern

Wyoming. Everything appeared as usual over the Tetons, but then, suddenly, there it was: the Yellowstone fire of 1988. Our flight path took us directly over the center of the fire. Passengers in the middle aisle rose hurriedly from their seats and crowded to the side windows. A stunned silence filled the cabin. Even from thirty-five thousand feet we could see the luminous walls of orange and red advancing through the thick forests. Black and gray and white smoke rose in opaque columns. Serpentine tentacles of fire probed the ridges and valleys, searching as if by intuitive sense for areas with accumulated dead wood and low ground moisture. I watched as many familiar places—Two Ocean Plateau, Heart Lake, Upper Geyser Basin, Mount Washburn, the Lamar Country—burned.

Although as a naturalist I understood the catastrophic fire was actually a good thing, and long overdue for the beautiful plateau, those around me viewed it with horror. In retrospect, the historic fire in the world's first national park provides a perfect metaphor and point of entry for this section of the book. Nature teaches, through forest fires and other natural disasters, that what appears to be destructive and negative can often be creative and beneficial. In the case of Yellowstone, a century of fire suppression had resulted in a million acres of trees weakened by disease, overcrowding, and insect infestations. The fire swept like strong medicine through the moribund stands, clearing out the dying and decayed trees, opening canopies, and bringing in sunlight to nourish the green plants that sustain the animal kingdom.

Since the fire I have returned four times to survey the Yellowstone landscape. I am continually amazed at the restorative powers of nature. And that is so often the deeper lesson of nature's fury—that in our universe destruction is powerfully wed to creation.

Nature, as we know her, is no saint.

—HENRY DAVID THOREAU, *ESSAYS*

———•◦•◦•———

The next day we got across [in the boat to Lower Mate-cumbe Key] and found things in terrible shape. Imagine you have read it in the papers but nothing could give an idea of the destruction. Between 700 and 1000 dead. Many, today, still unburied. The foliage absolutely stripped as though by fire for forty miles and the land looking like the abandoned bed of a river. Not a building of any sort standing. Over thirty miles of railway washed and blown away. We were the first in to Camp Five of the veterans who were working on the highway construction. Out of 187 only 8 survived. Saw more dead than I'd seen in one place since the Lower Piave in June of 1918.

—ERNEST HEMINGWAY, LETTER TO MAXWELL PERKINS FOLLOWING THE 1935 MATECUMBE HURRICANE IN THE FLORIDA KEYS, SEPTEMBER 7, 1935

Anyone who has tried to work effectively in −40 F weather, to contend with darkness in winter for long periods of time or the knife slash of windblown snow at these temperatures, wonders that any creature can endure like this for weeks on end, let alone seem to be at peace.

—BARRY LOPEZ, *ARCTIC DREAMS*

Out of the sun, the cold bit like ivory fangs.

—MAJORIE KINNAN RAWLINGS, *THE SOJOURNER*

A mature hurricane is by far the most powerful event on earth; the combined nuclear arsenals of the United States and the former Soviet Union don't contain enough energy to keep a hurricane going for one day.

—SEBASTIAN JUNGER, *THE PERFECT STORM*

The brig *St. John,* from Galway, Ireland, laden with emigrants, was wrecked [on Cape Cod] on Sunday morning; it was now Tuesday morning, and the sea was still breaking violently on the rocks. There were eighteen or twenty [caskets] lying on a green hillside, a few rods from the water, and surrounded by a crowd. The bodies which had been recovered, twenty-seven or eight in all, had been collected there . . . I saw many marble feet and matted heads as the cloths were raised, and one livid, swollen, and mangled body of a drowned girl, who probably had intended to go out to service in some American family.

—HENRY DAVID THOREAU, *CAPE COD*

Nature, to be commanded, must be obeyed.

—FRANCIS BACON, *ESSAYS*

The first impression that was made upon me when I landed on the wreck-strewn beach of the Place Bertin was one of loneliness, stillness, grayness, and almost unimaginable desolation. There was no color, no structural form, no traceable plan, and no sign whatever of recent life . . . One might have imagined that he was looking at the ruins of a big pueblo in an Arizona desert, which had been destroyed by a frightful earthquake a hundred years before. It was almost impossible to realize, or even to believe, that, within a month, this had been a bright, gay, beautiful city of thirty thousand inhabitants . . . It was often impossible for me to determine whether I was in a street or in the midst of a ruined block of building . . . the bodies of the dead were generally distorted and the color of burned coffee . . .

—GEORGE KENNAN, A MEMBER OF THE U.S. RELIEF EXPEDITION TO THE ISLAND OF MARTINIQUE FOLLOWING THE VOLCANIC ERUPTION OF 1902

The dangers of life are infinite, and safety is among
them.

—JOHANN WOLFGANG VON GOETHE, *ESSAYS*

———

And as the smart ship grew
In stature, grace, and hue,
In shadowy silent distance
grew the Iceberg too.

—THOMAS HARDY, "THE CONVERGENCE OF THE TWAIN"
(LINES ON THE LOSS OF THE *TITANIC*)

———

Powerful as our weapons are, vast as is the destruction
we are capable of, there is something still more powerful than we.

—JOSEPH WOOD KRUTCH, "ESSAY ON WILDERNESS"

Blow, winds, and crack your cheeks. Rage, blow.
You cataracts and hurricanes, spout
Till you have drenched our steeples, drowned the
   cocks.
You sulph'rous and thought-executing
   fires,
Vaunt couriers of oak-cleaving thunderbolts,
Singe my white head. And thou, all-shaking thunder,
Strike flat the thick rotundity o'th'world,
Crack Nature's moulds, all germains spill at once,
That makes ingrateful man.

—WILLIAM SHAKESPEARE, *KING LEAR*

The [monsoon] rain increases by the early morning, and
with trails [in the Himalayas] impassable, we shall remain
in this old cowshed. We live on an isle of canvas tenting
spread between the lines of leak, and spend most of a
dark day in sleeping bags, propped up against the wall.

—PETER MATTHIESSEN, *THE SNOW LEOPARD*

The shark swung over and the old man saw his eye was not alive and then he swung over once again, wrapping himself in two loops of the rope. The old man knew that he was dead but the shark would not accept it. Then, on his back, with his tail lashing and his jaws clicking, the shark plowed over the water as a speed-boat does . . . "He took about forty pounds," the old man said aloud. He took my harpoon too and all the rope, he thought, and now my fish bleeds again and there will be others . . ."But man is not made for defeat," he said."A man can be destroyed but not defeated."

—ERNEST HEMINGWAY, *THE OLD MAN AND THE SEA*

All collapsed, and the great shroud of the sea rolled on as it had five thousand years ago.

—HERMAN MELVILLE, *MOBY-DICK*

Every day we have been ready to start for our depot 11 miles away, but outside the door of our tent it remains a scene of whirling drift. I do not think we can hope for better things now. We shall stick it out to the end, but we are getting weaker, of course, and the end cannot be far. It seems a pity, but I do not think I can write more.

—JOURNAL OF ROBERT FALCON SCOTT, 1912,
SCOTT'S LAST EXPEDITION (TO THE SOUTH POLE)

Think of the storm roaming the sky uneasily like a dog looking for a place to sleep in, listen to it growling.

—ELIZABETH BISHOP, "LITTLE EXERCISE"

At 10:02 a series of terrific reports were heard, followed by a heavy black cloud rising up from the direction of Krakatoa Island, the barometer fell an inch at one jump, suddenly rising and falling an inch at a time, called all hands, furled all sails securely, which was scarcely done before the squall struck the ship with terrific force; let go port anchor and all the chain in the locker, wind increasing to a hurricane; let go starboard anchor . . . it was midnight at noon, a heavy shower of ashes coming with the squall, the air so thick it was difficult to breathe, also noticed a strong smell of sulphur, all hands expected to be suffocated; terrible noises from the volcano, the sky filled with forked lighting, running in all directions, the howling of the wind through the rigging formed one of the wildest and most awful scenes imaginable, all expecting that the last days of the earth had come; the water running by us in the direction of the volcano at the rate of 12 miles per hour . . .

—CAPTAIN'S LOG, USS *BESSE*, WHILE SAILING SEVERAL HUNDRED MILES NORTHEAST OF KRAKATOA, AUGUST 27, 1883

"The ship? Great God, where is the ship?"

—HERMAN MELVILLE, *MOBY-DICK* (LINES SPOKEN AFTER THE *PEQUOD* IS RAMMED AND SUNK BY A SPERM WHALE)

There Leviathan,
Hugest of living creatures, in the deep
Stretched like a promontory sleeps or swims,
And seems a moving land; and at his gills
Draws in, and at his breath spouts out a sea.

—JOHN MILTON, *PARADISE LOST*

And it was not the cold alone, though that could be brutal enough. Traveling on the river ice and in the creek bottoms, there was always danger of stepping into overflow water and getting wet to the skin. Many a far North trapper could tell of breaking through thin ice and plunging into knee-deep water, of the race to shore to build a fire, to warm and dry himself. If you got anything frozen out there, far from home and shelter, it was just too bad.

—JOHN HAINES, *THE STARS, THE SNOW, THE FIRE*

He pictured the boys finding his body next day. Suddenly he found himself with them, coming along the trail and looking for himself. He did not belong with himself any more, for he was out of himself, standing with the boys and looking at himself in the snow.

—JACK LONDON, "TO BUILD A FIRE"

It is only now and then, in a jungle, or amidst the towering white menace of a burnt or burning Australian forest, that Nature strips the moral veils from vegetation and we apprehend its stark ferocity.

—H.G. WELLS, "THE HAPPY TURNING"

I, an old man, have written this fire report. Among other things, it was important to me, as an exercise for old age, to enlarge my knowledge and spirit so I could accompany young men whose lives I might have lived on their way. I have climbed where they climbed, and in my time I have fought fire and inquired into its nature.

—NORMAN MACLEAN, *YOUNG MEN AND FIRE*

I was familiar with storms, and enjoyed them, knowing well that in right relations with them they are ever kindly.

—JOHN MUIR, "THE DISCOVERY OF GLACIER BAY"

The water is very swift and there is no landing-place. From around a curve there comes a mad roar, and down we are carried with a dizzying velocity to the head of another rapid. On either side high over our heads there are overhanging granite walls, and the sharp bends cut off our view, so that a few minutes will carry us into unknown waters. Away we go on one long, winding ride. I stand on deck, supporting myself with a strap fastened on either side of the gunwale. The boat glides rapidly where the water is smooth, then, striking a wave, she leaps and bounds like a thing of life, and we have a wild exhilarating ride for ten miles, which we make in less than an hour.

—JOHN WESLEY POWELL,
THE EXPLORATION OF THE COLORADO RIVER

They could trigger the EPIRB, but a night rescue in these conditions would be virtually impossible. They could deploy the life raft, but they probably wouldn't survive the huge seas. If the boat goes down, they go down with it, and no one on earth can do anything about it.

—SEBASTIAN JUNGER, *THE PERFECT STORM*

Surely, I thought, the storm would not last. The sun would come out and it would disappear swiftly, but instead the cold grew more intense, a wind came up, and the snow came down as heavily as before. By the end of the week there was a foot of it, and the singing [of the spring birds] became less and less noticeable . . . I picked up many that had died.

—SIGURD F. OLSON, "THE STORM"

Now let the howling winds of Pluto rise,
Destroy the engines of this singing world,
And send the shattered hulk, end over end,
Across the lonely gulfs of infinite space.

—NOH J. RAYMUR, *POEMS*

The sun was now so high, as to beam upon us with the same insufferable radiance of yesterday. The air which we inhaled, seemed to scald our lungs. [My companions] had so completely abandoned the hope of ever reaching the water that they threw themselves on the ground, resigned to die. I instantly determined to remain with my father, be it life or death.

—JAMES O. PATTIE, WRITING OF THE COLORADO DESERT IN HIS *PERSONAL NARRATIVE*

There is no sound but the crunch of boots on the sandy lane. And heavy breathing. The sweat drips from my hair down past my ears, from forehead into eyebrows and from there down around the corners of my eyes and along the nose.

—EDWARD ABBEY, ON HIS HISTORIC 110-MILE SOLO WALK ACROSS
THE SONORAN DESERT IN SOUTHWESTERN ARIZONA
(FROM "A WALK IN THE DESERT HILLS")

Desert is a loose term to indicate land that supports no man; whether the land can be bitten and broken to that purpose is not proven. Void of life it never is, however dry the air and villainous the soul.

—MARY AUSTIN, *THE LAND OF LITTLE RAIN*

The sun beats down with dead, blistering, relentless malignity; the perspiration is welling from every pore in man and beast, but scarcely a sign of it finds its way to the surface—it is absorbed before it gets there; there is not the faintest breath of air stirring; there is not a merciful shred of cloud in all the brilliant firmament; there is not a living creature visible in any direction; there is not a sound—not a sigh—not a whisper—not a buzz, or a whir of wings, or distant pipe of bird—not even a sob from the lost souls that doubtless peopled that dead air.

—MARK TWAIN, DESCRIBING THE GREAT BASIN DESERT, *ROUGHING IT*

Grass and sky were two canvases into which rich details painted and destroyed themselves with joyous intensity. As sunlight erases cloud, so fire ate grass and restored grass in a cycle of unrelenting power.

—LOUISE ERDRICH, "BIG GRASS"

The second before the sun went out we saw a wall of dark shadow come speeding at us. We no sooner saw it than it was upon us, like thunder . . . It was as if an enormous, loping god in the sky had reached down and slapped the earth's face.

—ANNIE DILLARD, "TOTAL ECLIPSE"

Be like the promontory against which the waves continually break, but it stands firm and tames the fury of the water around it.

—MARCUS AURELIUS, *MEDITATION*

Beauty

This is the most beautiful place on earth. There are many such places. Every man, every woman, carries in heart and mind the image of the ideal place, the right place, the one true home, known or unknown, actual or visionary.

—EDWARD ABBEY, WRITING OF ARCHES NATIONAL PARK IN *DESERT SOLITAIRE*

The artist Georgia O'Keeffe always comes to mind on the subject of beauty, and not simply because her paintings are so strongly associated with the beauty of one place—her adobe home and the surrounding countryside in northern New Mexico.

One story about O'Keeffe and her appreciation of beauty regards a rafting trip she and landscape photographer Eliot Porter took down the San Juan River. During the journey Eliot Porter found an unusually beautiful river stone. It was worn glassy smooth by the current and possessed striking colors. O'Keeffe, who kept a large bowl of riverstones in her studio, asked Porter if she could have the stone and he said no, having already hatched a plan. A few months later, Porter invited O'Keeffe over for dinner at his home in Santa Fe and placed the stone in a conspicuous location. After O'Keeffe went home that night Porter and his wife observed that—sure enough— the stone had disappeared. According to her biographer, Roxanne Robinson, O'Keeffe later used the river stone as the visual source for one of her most distinctive paintings.

Beside the futon on which I sleep each night are about a dozen smooth stones. Each stone comes from a different place. There is an angular fragment of dense-grained greenstone from a tundra ridge in the Alaska Range, a small moon-colored geode from a nameless canyon in southern Utah, a chunk of black marble from the Mojave desert, an oblong egg of blue turquoise from a dry wash in Arizona, a sea-washed matrix of crystal and quartzite from a pebbled cove in California, a milky agate from an aspen-covered mountain in western Colorado. And several others, each from a different place, each well worn from human touch.

Each night, before I go to sleep, I take one of these stones into my hand. I call them dreamstones. As I grasp the stone I recall the beautiful place from which it came. By degrees I am transported there, to the quiet solitude of a desert dune field, or to a peaceful beach on the Big Sur coast, or to an arctic mountaintop on which a herd of caribou graze.

These stones represent my special places. These stones, and the beautiful places they evoke, are a part of what I live for and a part of what I carry with me every day. Such is the power of beauty to stir the spirit and enrich the journey of life.

I loved it immediately. From then on I was always on my way back . . . It was a perfectly mad looking country—hills and cliffs and washes too crazy to imagine all thrown up into the air by God and let tumble where they would. It was certainly as spectacular as anything I'd ever seen—and that was pretty good—the evening glow on a cliff in a vast sort of red and gold and purple amphitheater while we sat on our horse on top of a hill of the whitish green earth.

—GEORGIA O'KEEFFE, WRITING OF NEW MEXICO

I believe the world is incomprehensibly beautiful—an endless prospect of magic and wonder.

—ANSEL ADAMS, COMMENCEMENT ADDRESS, OCCIDENTAL COLLEGE, JUNE 1961

Though we travel the world over to find the beautiful, we must carry it with us or we find it not.

—RALPH WALDO EMERSON, "BEAUTY"

In the house of long life I live,
In the house of happiness, there I wander.
Beauty before me, with it I wander.
Beauty behind me, with it I wander.
Beauty below me, with it I wander,
Beauty above me, with it I wander.
Beauty all around me, with it I wander.
In old age travelling, with it I wander.
On the beautiful trail I am, with it I wander.

—DAWN BOY'S SONG ON ENTERING WHITE HOUSE,
NAVAJO MYTHS, PRAYERS AND SONGS

A nobler want of man is served by nature, namely, the love of Beauty.

—RALPH WALDO EMERSON, "BEAUTY"

A thing of beauty is a joy for ever;
its loveliness increases; it will never
Pass into nothingness; but still will keep
A bower quiet for us, and a sleep
Full of sweet dreams, and health, and quiet breathing.

      —JOHN KEATS, "ENDYMION"

"Beauty is truth, truth beauty,"—that is all ye know on
earth, and all ye need to know.

      —JOHN KEATS, "ODE ON A GRECIAN URN"

What is beautiful is good and who is good will soon also
be beautiful.

      —SAPPHO, FRAGMENTS

There are times of great beauty on a coffee-farm. When the plantation flowered in the beginning of the rains, it was a radiant sight, like a cloud of chalk, in the mist and the drizzling rain, over six hundred acres of land.

—ISAK DINESEN, *OUT OF AFRICA*

I don't see that I could survive if I wasn't actively engaged in trying to make something beautiful.

—BARRY LOPEZ, *THE BLOOMSBURY REVIEW* INTERVIEW, 1988

Those things are better which are perfected by nature than those which are finished by art.

—CICERO, "PRO ARCHIA POETA"

Beauty has a short-lived reign.

—SOCRATES, AS QUOTED BY DIOGENES LAERTIUS

I think that I shall never see
A billboard lovely as a tree.
Indeed, unless the billboards fall
I'll never see a tree at all.

—OGDEN NASH, "SONG OF THE OPEN ROAD"

The beauty of the natural world lies in the details . . .

—NATALIE ANGIER, THE BEAUTY OF THE BEASTLY

When I heard the learn'd astronomer,
When the proofs, the figures, were ranged in columns
    before me,
When I was shown the charts and diagrams, to add,
    divide, and measure them,
When I sitting heard the astronomer where he lectured
    with much applause in the lecture-room,
How soon unaccountable I became tired and sick,
Till rising and gliding out I wander'd off by myself,
In the mystical moist night air, and from time to time,
Look'd up in perfect silence at the stars.

—WALT WHITMAN, "WHEN I HEARD THE LEARN'D ASTRONOMER"

Loveliest of trees, the cherry now
Is hung with bloom along the bough,
And stands about the woodland ride
Wearing a white for Eastertide.

Now of my threescore years and ten,
Twenty will not come again,
And take from seventy springs a score,
It only leaves me twenty more.

And since to look at things in bloom
Fifty springs are little room,
About the woodland I will go
To see the cherry hung with snow.

—A. E. HOUSMAN, "LOVELIEST OF TREES"

Beauty has as many meanings as man has moods.
    Beauty is the symbol of symbols.
Beauty reveals everything, because it expresses nothing.
When it shows us itself, it shows us the whole fiery-
    colored world.

    —Oscar Wilde, "The Critic as Artist"

Everything has beauty, but not everyone sees it.

    —Confucius

It is a beauteous evening, calm and free,
The holy time is quiet as a Nun
Breathless with adoration; the broad sun
Is sinking down in its tranquility . . .

    —William Wordsworth, "It is a Beauteous Evening"

It was spring in Paris and everything looked just a little too beautiful.

—ERNEST HEMINGWAY, "BULL FIGHTING A TRAGEDY,"
TORONTO STAR WEEKLY, October 20, 1923

Whenever I go down into this magical zone of the low water of the spring tides, I look for the most delicately beautiful of all the shore's inhabitants—flowers that are not plant but animal, blooming on the threshold of the deeper sea. Hanging from its roof were the pendent flowers of the hydroid Tubularia, pale, pink, fringed and delicate as the wind flower. Here were creatures so exquisitely fashioned that they seemed unreal, their beauty too fragile to exist in a world of crushing force.

—RACHEL CARSON, *THE EDGE OF THE SEA*

Thunderstorms are spectacular and beautiful up in the jagged rocky peaks.

—Rick Bass, "Magic at Ruth Lake"

The most natural beauty in the world is honesty and moral truth. For all beauty is truth.

—Anthony Ashely Cooper, Third Earl of Shaftsbury, "Freedom of Wit and Humour"

Nature cannot be surprised in undress. Beauty breaks in everywhere.

—Ralph Waldo Emerson, "Beauty"

Beauty varies with the time of life.

—Aristotle, *Metaphysics*, Book XIII

He who has been instructed thus far in the things of love, and who has learned to see the beautiful in due order and succession, when he comes toward the end will suddenly perceive a nature of wondrous beauty (and this, Socrates, is the final cause of all our former toils)— a nature which in the first place is everlasting, not growing and decaying, or waxing and waning . . . but beauty absolute, separate, simple, and everlasting, which without diminution and without increase, or any change, is imparted to the ever-growing and perishing beauty of all other things . . . And the true order of thinking . . . is to begin from the beauties of earth and mount upwards for the sake of that other beauty . . . "This, my dear Socrates," said the stranger of Mantineia, "is that life above all others which man should live, in the contemplation of beauty absolute."

—PLATO, SYMPOSIUM 210

Every single story that nature tells is gorgeous.

—NATALIE ANGIER, *THE BEAUTY OF THE BEASTLY*

When I detect a beauty in any of the recesses of nature, I am reminded, by the serene and retired spirit in which it requires to be contemplated, of the inexpressible privacy of a life,—how silent and unambitious it is. The beauty there is in mosses must be considered from the holiest, quietest nook.

—HENRY DAVID THOREAU, "NATURAL HISTORY OF MASSACHUSETTS"

I sat some minutes, lost in my thoughts of the beauty of the place.

—WILLIAM O. DOUGLAS, "THE MAROON BELLS OF COLORADO" (FROM *MY WILDERNESS*)

Words are inadequate to describe the flight [of migrating cranes], the many variations in the formations, the alternate beating of wings and sailing, the beauty of the flocks in silhouettes against the white mountain [Denali] and the blue sky, and the exhilarating poetry of it all in this primeval wilderness country.

—ADOLPH MURIE, *A NATURALIST IN ALASKA*

Beauty without grace is the hook without the bait.

—RALPH WALDO EMERSON, "BEAUTY"

The [mud] flats [of Cape Cod] hold a subtle, rather than an obvious beauty. It is the beauty of uncountable gradation of tone and hue, of the sheen and polish of exposed wet sand at low water. It is a world of reflections upon the wet sand from the slanted light of the morning sky.

—CLARE LEIGHTON, *WHERE LAND MEETS THE SEA*

The wilderness was a beautiful, even enchanting place
with its graceful movement and active life.

—SALLY CARRIGHAR, *HOME TO THE WILDERNESS*

—————

Out of all the cold darkness and glacial crushing and
grinding comes this warm, abounding beauty and life to
teach us that what we in our faithless ignorance and
fear call destruction is creation finer and finer.

—JOHN MUIR, *TRAVELS IN ALASKA*

—————

It is, I have always said, paradise on earth.

—JANE GOODALL, WRITING OF THE GOMBE NATIONAL PARK IN
TANZANIA IN HER ESSAY "DIGGING UP THE ROOTS"

Liberation

I would rather be ashes than dust! I would rather that my spark should burn out in a brilliant blaze than it should be stifled by dry-rot. I would rather be a superb meteor, every atom of me in magnificent glow, than a sleepy and permanent planet. The function of man is to live, not to exist. I shall not waste my days trying to prolong them. I shall use my time.

—ATTRIBUTED TO JACK LONDON TWO WEEKS BEFORE HIS DEATH, 1916

Henry David Thoreau built his legendary cabin at Walden Pond. His year-long exile from Concord was a deliberate exercise in independence and self-sufficiency, as well as a quiet revolution against the stifling strictures of New England Puritanism. It also had something to do with getting over the death of his brother.

Similarly, Theodore Roosevelt departed the comforts of plutocratic New York following the deaths of his wife and mother and created a rugged new life for himself at the Elkhorn Ranch. On the wild western frontier he was freed—both figuratively and literally—from the burden of the past.

Liberation for most of us takes a simpler, although by no means less important, form. We drive through the gates at the Conservancy's Pine Butte Swamp Preserve near Choteau, Montana, for example, and spot a pronghorn antelope, and then a pair of mule deer, and then perhaps a herd of elk. The sky is high and blue, the clouds are slow and lazy, the day has endless possibilities. On entering the preserve—on entering any nature sanctuary—we notice a few striking changes. The sweat-stained hat is pushed back far on the head. A deep satisfied breath is drawn. An involuntary smile forms. Perhaps, if no one is around, a rebel yell is heard emanating from our general direction. Why? Because we have suddenly, in a sense, become free. We are, in a word, liberated. In these wild places we can see the world as it was thousands of years ago, before tribal clans, before permanent villages, before city-states and regional states and nation states. We can, more fundamentally, see the landscape as it was when we were children—endless and unclaimed, belonging to everyone, and to no one.

Be joyful because it is humanly possible.

—WENDELL BERRY, "NOTES FOR AN ABSENCE AND A RETURN"

The land is love.

—TERRY TEMPEST WILLIAMS, "WINTER SOLSTICE AT THE MOAB SLOUGH

Bread feeds the body indeed, but flowers feed also the soul.

—THE KORAN

From this hour I ordain myself loos'd of limits and imaginary lines,
Going where I list, my own master, total and absolute.

—WALT WHITMAN, "SONG OF THE OPEN ROAD"

He who knows the most; he who knows what sweets and virtues are in the ground, the water, the plants, the heavens, and how to come at these enchantments, is the rich and royal man.

—RALPH WALDO EMERSON, *Essays*

The mood in which you set out on a spring or autumn ramble or a sturdy winter walk, and your greedy feet have to be restrained from devouring the distances too fast, is the mood in which your best thoughts and impulses come to you, or in which you might embark on any noble and heroic enterprise. Life is sweet in such moods, the universe is complete, and there is no failure or imperfection anywhere.

—JOHN BURROUGHS, *Pepacton*

Of what avail are forty freedoms without a blank spot on the map?

—ALDO LEOPOLD, "THE GREEN LAGOONS"

By eight o'clock everything was ready and we were on the other side of the river. We jumped into the stage-coach, the driver cracked his whip, and we bowled away and left "the States" behind us. It was a superb summer morning, and all the landscape was brilliant with sunshine. There was a freshness and breeziness, too, and an exhilarating sense of emancipation from all sorts of cares and responsibilities that almost made us feel that the years we had spent in the close, hot city, toiling and slaving, had been wasted and thrown away. We were spinning along through Kansas, and in the course of an hour and a half we were fairly abroad on the great plains.

—MARK TWAIN, *ROUGHING IT*

There is a rapture on the lonely shore,
There is society, where none intrudes,
By the deep sea, and music in its roar.

—LORD BYRON, *CHILDE HAROLD'S PILGRIMAGE*

My angel—his name is Freedom—
Choose him to be your King;
He shall cut pathways east and west,
And fend you with his wing.

—RALPH WALDO EMERSON, "BOSTON HYMN"

Freedom is the will to be responsible to ourselves.

—FREDERICK NIETZSCHE, *TWILIGHT OF THE IDOLS*

Nature, like liberty, is but restrained
By the same laws which first herself ordained.

—ALEXANDER POPE, "AN ESSAY ON CRITICISM"

This is a delicious evening, when the whole body is one sense, and imbibes delight through every pore. I go and come with a strange liberty in Nature, a part of herself.

—HENRY DAVID THOREAU, *WALDEN*

In the woods, too, a man casts off his years, as the snake his slough, and at what period soever of life is always a child. In the woods is perpetual youth.

—RALPH WALDO EMERSON, *NATURE*

I have stopped sleeping inside. A house is too small, too confining. I want the whole world, and the stars too.

—SUE HUBBELL, *A COUNTRY YEAR*

I wish to speak a word for Nature, for absolute freedom and wildness, as contrasted with a freedom and culture merely civil,—to regard man as an inhabitant, or a part and parcel of Nature, rather than a member of society. I wish to make an extreme statement, if so I may make an emphatic one, for there are enough champions of civilization: the minister and the school-committee and every one of you will take care of that.

—HENRY DAVID THOREAU, "WALKING"

Freedom of the wilderness means many things to different people. If you really want to enjoy it, you must recognize your responsibilities as adult humans living in a world with others . . . Freedom gives no one license to change a heritage that belongs to the ages.

—SIGURD F. OLSON, *REFLECTIONS FROM THE NORTH COUNTRY*

When I first came down to the city from my mountain home, I began to wither, and wish instinctively for the vital woods and high sky. Yet I lingered month after month, plodding at "duty." At length I chanced to see a lovely goldenrod in bloom in a weedy spot alongside one of the less frequented sidewalks there. Suddenly I was aware of the ending of summer and fled. Then, once away, I saw how shrunken and lean I was and how glad I was I had gone [back to the wilderness].

—JOHN MUIR, *JOURNALS*

I like to sit there above the mint fields and feel my soul cutting down through the bedrock. It's happening fast. I too am becoming the earth.

—RICK BASS, "ON WILLOW CREEK"

The mystery of language was revealed to me. I knew then that "w-a-t-e-r" meant the wonderful cool something that was flowing over my hand. That living world awakened my soul, gave it light, joy, set it free!

—HELEN KELLER, STORY OF MY LIFE

If you want to see birds, you must have birds in your heart.

—JOHN BURROUGHS, OUTSIDE MAGAZINE

My heart is like a singing bird.

—CHRISTINA ROSSETTI, "A BIRTHDAY"

When you reach the top, keep climbing.

—ZEN PROVERB

I don't want to get to the end of my life and find that I've just lived the length of it. I want to have lived the width of it as well.

—DIANE ACKERMAN, *NEWSWEEK* MAGAZINE

Freed from the pressure of haste ... I found myself looking more closely at what went on around me.

—COLIN FLETCHER, *THE MAN WHO WALKED THROUGH TIME*

How free are the wild geese on their wings,
And the rest they find on the thick Yu trees,
But we, ceaseless toilers in the king's services,
Cannot even plant our millet and rice.

—CHINESE SHI-CHING, *BOOK OF ODES*

A great work of fiction can become a cornerstone . . . for all manners of ideas, such as the importance of wildness and wilderness, or concepts of grace, freedom, liberty.

—RICK BASS, *THE BOOK OF YAAK*

In a few weeks I must go back to the city and take up my work . . . Here in the quiet of the woods I am trying to take stock of all that this year has done for me. It has given me health. I have forgotten about jerking nerves and aching muscles. I sleep all night like a stone; I eat plain food with relish; I walk and row mile after mile; I work rejoicing in my strength and glad to be alive.

—LAURA LEE DAVIDSON, *A WINTER OF CONTENT*

While my interest in natural history has added very little to my sum of achievement, it has added immeasurably to my sum of enjoyment in life.

—THEODORE ROOSEVELT, "MY LIFE AS A NATURALIST"

This is happiness: to be dissolved into something completely great.

—WILLA CATHER, *MY ANTONIA*

I stand on the edge of these wetlands, a place of renewal, an oasis in the desert, as an act of faith believing
the sun has completed the southern end of its journey
and is now contemplating its return toward light.

—TERRY TEMPEST WILLIAMS, "WINTER SOLSTICE AT THE MOAB
SLOUGH"

Something will have gone out of us as a people if we
ever let the remaining wilderness be destroyed . . . [for]
the wilderness [is] the thing that has helped to make an
American different from, and, until we forget it in the
roar of our industrial cities, more fortunate than other
men. For an American, insofar as he is new and different at all, is a civilized man who has renewed himself in
the wild.

—WALLACE STEGNER, "WILDERNESS LETTER"

Seasons

Now every field, now every tree is green,
And friendly nature's fairest face is seen.
—VIRGIL, *ECLOGUES III*, V. 56

From an early age the four great seasons of fall, winter, spring, and summer lay the fundamental groundwork for our lives. Even by the age of ten, for example, my best friend and I had learned the progression of wildflowers around our boyhood homes in southwestern Ohio. First to come, as early as the second week in March, were the familiar white blossoms of the spring beauty, each flower delicately veined in pink. Within a few days the purple violets would form masses on the forest floor, always thickest where the snows had been deepest. This was followed in turn by such famous Midwestern beauties as bloodroot, anemone, hepatica, yellow adder's tongue, and trillium. Last and most lovely to arrive at the party were the Dutchman's breeches, each slender stalk of cream-colored flowers nestled in its own basket of lacy green leaves. Above it all, the forest trees would begin to bud and blossom and the songbirds—this was before migratory songbirds became scarce—would sing so loudly at sunrise it would be impossible to sleep.

Summertime found the forest canopy thick and the wild roses and black-eyed Susans blossoming in the clearings. The hot days of July were the prime snake-hunting season. Whole days were spent wading the streams and stalking the meadows, often returning with reluctant new specimens for our unlicensed "zoo." The wild raspberries and blackberries would be ripe by mid-August, and by the time of the first school exams we could begin to seriously harvest our backyard gardens—everything from artichokes to zucchini. Some years the fall colors were lovely, with the leaves lingering into early November. Late bloomers such as the purple aster could often be found past Thanksgiving, if a person knew where to look. I can recall energetic woodland battles with buckeyes and osage oranges, our breath frosting the air as we hid in the blue shadows. Winter was a good time for sledding. On clear nights we would carry our mail-order telescopes to a nearby hill and study such mysterious objects as the Pleiades, or the

Seven Sisters, in the constellation Orion. The planet Mars, we had learned by then, also had four seasons.

Now, as I write this, it is winter. We've had a two-week cold snap (−19°F!) followed by a welcome thaw, a wild, warm chinook gusting across the prairie from the mountains, the air full of rich earth scents and stirring first thoughts of spring. It is the day after Christmas. It will be cold again, to be sure, and snows will bring the cooing pigeons back to the porch, but already I am unrolling my topographic maps and making plans for my annual spring trip to the Painted Desert, and thinking ahead to a summer of outdoor activities with my son, and then to my yearly fall trip to Jackson Hole and Yellowstone. What the seasons have most taught me over the last forty-four years is that you must embrace the changes of this world.

To everything there is a season, and a time to every
    purpose under the heaven; A time
to be born, and a time to die; a time to plant, and a time
    to pluck up that which is
planted; A time to kill, and a time to heal; A time to
    break down and a time to build up;
A time to cast away stones, and a time to gather stones
    together; a time to embrace and
a time to refrain from embracing; A time to get and A
    time to lose; a time to keep and
a time to cast away; A time to rend, and a time to sew;
    A time to keep silence, and a
time to speak; A time to love, and a time to hate; A time
    of war, and a time of peace.

> —ECCLESIASTES (LATER INSPIRED THE LYRICS FOR "TURN, TURN,
> TURN," A HIT SONG BY ROGER MCGUINN AND THE ROCK AND ROLL
> BAND THE BYRDS IN THE 1960S)

He loved the hills in the spring when the snows go off and the first flowers come. He loved the warm sun of summer and the high mountain meadows, the trails through the timber and the sudden clear blue of the lakes. Best of all he loved the fall, with the tawny, and gray, the leaves yellow on the cottonwoods and above the hills the high blue windless skies.

—ERNEST HEMINGWAY, GRAVESIDE EULOGY FOR HIS
HUNTING FRIEND GENE VAN GUILDER, SUN VALLEY, IDAHO,
NOVEMBER 3, 1939

The bright days of Indian summer are choice along the Potomac. Maples are crimson; sumac and dogwood, a rich dark red; gum trees and paw paw, yellow; willow oak, a dull gold. There are fall days when the leaves have not yet fallen and when no breeze touches the trees. Then it's as if the woods were holding their breath, lest a leaf be lost.

—WILLIAM O. DOUGLAS, *MY WILDERNESS*

There is a midsummer. There is a midwinter. But there is no midspring or midautumn. These are seasons of constant change. Like dawn and dusk they are periods of transition. But like night and day and day and night they merge slowly, gradually.

—EDWIN WAY TEALE, *AUTUMN ACROSS AMERICA*

When there is no month in which flowers do not bloom, one can only consult the almanac or the sky if one insists upon establishing a fixed point.

—JOSEPH WOOD KRUTCH, *THE DESERT YEAR*

Like the swarms of clustering bees that pour forth in
fresh bursts from the cleft in the stone wall; and hang
like bunched fruit as they hover beneath the flowers in
spring-time, drifting in swarms together this way and
that way, so the many nations of men from the ships
and the shelters along the front of the wide ocean beach
marched in order by companies to the assembly area . . .

—HOMER, *THE ILIAD*, BOOK II

Blasted with sighs, and surrounded with tears,
Hither I come to seek the spring,
And at mine eyes, and at mine ears,
Receive such balms as else cure everything.

—JOHN DONNE, "TWICKNAM GARDEN"

The spring affords to a mind, so free from the distur-
bance of cares or passions as to be vacant to calm
amusements, almost everything that our present state
makes us capable of enjoying.

—SAMUEL JOHNSON, RAMBLER NO. 5 ("ON SPRING")

It is the first mild day of March:
Each minute sweeter than before,
The redbreast sings from the tall larch
That stands beside our door.

—WILLIAM WORDSWORTH, "TO MY SISTER"

The green paths down the hillsides are channels for streams. The young wheat is streaked by silver lines of water running between the ridges, the sheep are gathered together on the slopes. After the wet dark days, the country seems more populous. It peoples itself in the sunbeams. The garden, mimic of spring, is gay with flowers.

—DOROTHY WORDSWORTH, *JOURNAL*

———

The Crow will tumble up and down
At the first sight of spring
And in old trees around the town
Brush winter from its wing.

—JOHN CLARE, "CROWS IN SPRING"

When lilacs last in the dooryard bloom'd,
And the great star early droop'd in the western sky in
the night,
I mourn'd, and yet shall mourn with ever-returning
spring . . .

—WALT WHITMAN, "WHEN LILACS LAST IN THE DOORYARD
BLOOM'D" (AN ELEGY FOR ABRAHAM LINCOLN)

April is the cruelest month.

—T. S. ELIOT, "THE WASTE LAND"

To those who observe nature from day to day, the coming of spring is announced first of all by more light. The
country folk then say that the bear is turning over in his
lair; the sun is smiling ever brighter, and though more
frosts are ahead, the Gypsy sells his sheepskin.

—MIKHAIL PRISHVIN, NATURE'S DIARY

One swallow does not make a summer, but one skein of geese, cleaving the murk of a March thaw, is the spring.

—ALDO LEOPOLD, *A SAND COUNTY ALMANAC*

———

October to April is a long time. But there is a great compensation. Spring in the North comes with a leap and a shout and a surge of excitement. The change begins in February, the month of the returning sun, with glorious sunsets and a softening of the air. In March all the dog mushers are burned to a deep brown by the intense sun reflected from the snow. In April the snow, never very deep in interior Alaska, is going away fast and it is daylight-dusky nearly all night.

—MARGARET MURIE, *TWO IN THE FAR NORTH*

To anyone who has spent a winter in the north and known the depths to which the snow can reach, known the weeks when the mercury stays below zero, the first hint of spring is a major event.

—SIGURD F. OLSON, *THE SINGING WILDERNESS*

Spring is in the air. The breeze is gentle with the smell of birthing, the earth radiates freshness, the birds sing with more abandon than they have for months.

—BARBARA DEAN, *WELLSPRING*

Though a country be split in two, hills and rivers
    endure;
And spring comes green again to trees and grasses . . .

—TU FU, "A SPRING VIEW"

Late spring, the season of romping and romance.
—Jan DeBlieu, *Hatteras Journal*

In those vernal seasons of the year, when the air is calm and pleasant, it were an injury and sullenest against Nature not to go out and see her riches, and partake in her rejoicing with heaven and earth.
—John Milton, *Tractate of Education*

Summer afternoon—summer afternoon; to me those have always been the two most beautiful words in the English language.
—Henry James, as quoted in *A Backward Glance* by Edith Wharton

How sweet I roamed from field to field,
And tasted all the summer's pride.

—WILLIAM BLAKE, "SONG"

At midnight, in the month of June,
I stand beneath the mystic moon . . .

—EDGAR ALLAN POE, "THE SLEEPER"

It was a beautiful July day, one of those days which occur only when the weather has been unchanged for a long time.

—IVAN TURGENEV, *SKETCHES FROM A HUNTER'S ALBUM*

The drowsy heat of middle August lay heavy as a fur robe on the upper country of the Shell River, the North Platte of the white man. Almost every noon the thunder built themselves a dark cloud to ride the far crown of Laramie Peak.

—MARI SANDOZ, *CRAZY HORSE*

Late in August the lure of the mountains becomes
    irresistible.

—EDWARD ABBEY, *DESERT SOLITAIRE*

That time of year thou mayst in me behold
When yellow leaves, or none, or few, do hang
Upon those boughs which shake against the cold
Bare ruined choirs where late the sweet birds sang . . .

—WILLIAM SHAKESPEARE, SONNET LXXIII

But see the fading many-colour'd Woods,
Shade deepening over Shade; the Country round
Imbrown; a crouded Umbrage, dusk, and dun,
Of every Hue, from wan declining Green
To sooty Dark.

—JAMES THOMSON, "AUTUMN"

The trees are in their autumn beauty,
The woodland paths are dry,
Under the October twilight the water
Mirrors a still sky;
Upon the brimming water among the stones
Are nine-and-fifty swans . . .

—WILLIAM BUTLER YEATS, "THE WILD SWANS AT COOLE"

Season of mists and mellow fruitfulness,
Close bosom-friend of the maturing sun;
Conspiring with him how to load and bless
With fruit the vines that round the thatch-eves run;
To bend with apples the moss'd cottage-trees,
And fill all fruit with ripeness to the core;
To swell the gourd, and plump the hazel shells
With a sweet kernel; to set budding more,
And still more, later flowers for the bees,
Until they think warm days will never cease,
For Summer has o'er-brimmed their clammy cells . . .

—JOHN KEATS, "TO AUTUMN"

Some trees, as small hickories, appear to have dropped their leaves instantaneously, as a soldier grounds arms at a signal; and those of the hickory, being bright yellow still, though withered, reflect a blaze of light from the ground where they lie. Down they have come on all sides, at the first earnest touch of autumn's wand, making a sound like rain.

—HENRY DAVID THOREAU, "AUTUMNAL TINTS"

After rain the empty mountain
Stands autumnal in the evening,
Moonlight falls among the pines
And lays across the quiet streams.
Bamboos whisper of days long past,
Lotus-leaves yield before a sudden wind,
What does it matter that springtime has gone,
While you are here, my old friend?

—WANG WEI, "AUTUMN EVENING IN THE MOUNTAINS"

Now in November comes the sun down the abandoned
heaven.

    —D. H. Lawrence, "November by the Sea"

My Sorrow, when she's here with me,
Thinks these dark days of autumn rain
Are beautiful as days can be;
She loves the bare, the withered tree;
She walks the sodden pasture lane.

    —Robert Frost, "My November Guest"

Often the rainy season finds its terrible climax in September or October, in the crashing impact of a hurricane, the true cyclonic storm of the tropics.

    —Marjory Stoneman Douglas, *The Everglades*

When forty winters shall besiege thy brow
And dig deep trenches in thy beauty's field
Thy youth's proud livery, so gazed on now,
Will be a tottered weed of small worth held . . .

—WILLIAM SHAKESPEARE, SONNET I

Blow, blow, thou winter wind,
Thou art not so unkind
As man's ingratitude.

—WILLIAM SHAKESPEARE, SONG FROM *AS YOU LIKE IT*

Nature is full of genius, full of the divinity; so that not a snowflake escapes its fashioning hand.

—HENRY DAVID THOREAU, *JOURNAL*

Announced by all the trumpets of the sky,
Arrives the snow.

—RALPH WALDO EMERSON, "THE SNOWSTORM"

The Frost performs its secret ministry,
  Unhelped by any wind.

—SAMUEL TAYLOR COLERIDGE, "FROST AT MIDNIGHT"

There's a certain slant of light,
Winter afternoons,
That oppresses, like the heft
Of cathedral tunes . . .

—EMILY DICKINSON, POEM 258

The sun that brief December day
Rose cheerless over hills of gray . . .

—JOHN GREENLEAF WHITTIER, "SNOW-BOUND"

Sometimes in the mornings the frost lay white-grained on the grass. The wild plums that hung rich and ready on the Yellowstone had petered out, along with the salt weed that kept the horses stout in wintertime.

—A. B. GUTHRIE JR., THE BIG SKY

For some time now in the woods, away from the sun, in ravines and hollows where the ground is normally wet, the soil has darkened and is hard and cold to the touch. The deep, shaded mosses have stiffened, and there are tiny crystals of ice in their hairy spaces.

—JOHN HAINES, "ICE"

It was still hot back in Mississippi and in Texas, where I used to live, but it was already cold in the mountains, up in the North, in this place where I was going to start a new life. The immediate, pressing problem, I realized, was that winter was perhaps a month away. I knew nothing about winter. I had never seen it before, and I felt dizzy with fear, giddy with wonder, anticipating it.

—RICK BASS, *WINTER*

—•+•+•—

After two nights without a freeze the maple seeds began to sprout on the slope by the pond in the woods.

—DIANA KAPPEL-SMITH, *WINTERING*

Mystery

We all continually move on the edges of eternity, and are sometimes granted vistas through the fabric of illusion.

—ANSEL ADAMS, *AUTOBIOGRAPHY*

Even after forty years, I can recall the first mystery. It was summer and my brothers and I and were playing in the backyard sandbox at our home. We were building an elaborate medieval castle, complete with a water-filled moat. Suddenly there was a steady dull roaring in the sky, a strange harsh sound like nothing we had ever heard before. We looked up, in all the innocence of childhood, our faces blank with puzzlement. What we saw was a paradox. It was an airplane, but it had no propellers. It had wings, but they were swept back at an angle. It was maintaining flight, but it was traveling much too fast. We understood how airplanes worked from our rubber-band gliders, but this new object was a mystery. It literally seemed to us that the poor crippled thing would drop from the clouds at any moment. We followed it across the sky until it disappeared, and then we couldn't stop talking about it. What we had just seen, we learned later, was the first commercial jet airliner to land at the Greater Cincinnati Airport.

Mysteries fill our world. They come in any category you wish—politics, sports, entertainment, science, history, and of course, nature. There is a whole taxonomy to the subject of mysteries, ranging from the mundane to the weighty.

On the afternoon my mother died, for example, I asked the cardiac surgeon, "What do you think happened?" He shrugged his shoulders. It could have been a problem with the potassium levels, or the electrolytes, or maybe a clot in the graft. He didn't know, or if he did know, he wasn't saying. It will remain a mystery.

I can also think of mysteries that were solved. Once in Denali National Park I saw a pack of wolves behaving unusually. As I approached them on the tundra of Thorofare Pass they did not turn and walk away, as wolves normally do, but began pacing back and forth nervously and howling. I decided to leave them alone and later described the observation to a park naturalist, who explained that the mother wolf of the Toklat pack had given birth out on the open tundra, far from the natal den, and that the rest of the pack was bringing her food each day. The wolves had been trying to protect their secret.

Many times out in the desert I have walked away from the campfire and gazed up at the stars and wondered about the great mysteries. How did life begin? What is life? In what direction will human life evolve?

I, for one, am glad for so many questions, happy for so many mysteries. They form the boundaries of our world. Without them, without the unknown, life would be borderless and absurd. We would have no reason to exist, for there would be nothing left to know. Some say that there are fewer mysteries now than in antiquity, but it has often struck me that the opposite is true—that the more we probe, the more we find, and that the universe becomes more immense, and more beautiful in that enormity, with each new discovery. It is one thing, for example, to look at a map of the desert. It is quite another to start walking across it and see how truly vast it is.

The eternal mystery of the world is its
  comprehensibility.

—ALBERT EINSTEIN, *OUT OF MY LATER YEARS*

There are more things on heaven and earth
Than are dreamt of in your philosophy, Horatio.

—WILLIAM SHAKESPEARE, *HAMLET*

Is there some significance here I am unaware of? Or no
significance at all?

—CZESLAW MILOSZ, 1980 NOBEL LAUREATE IN LITERATURE,
SYMBOLIC MOUNTAINS AND FORESTS

Men perish because they cannot join the beginning
  with the end.

—ALCMAEON OF CROTONA

Everything flows and nothing abides; everything gives
way and nothing stays fixed.

—HERACLEITUS OF EPHESUS

The Sea
Isn't a place
But a fact, and
a mystery

—MARY OLIVER, "THE WAVES"

"I want to know what it says. The sea, Floy, what is it
that it keeps on saying?"

—CHARLES DICKENS, *DOMBEY AND SON*

Each time I look up one of the secretive little side canyons I half expect to see not only the cottonwood tree over its tiny spring—the leafy god, the desert's liquid eye—but also a rainbow-colored corona of blazing light, pure spirit, pure being, pure disembodied intelligence about to speak my name. If a man's imagination were not so weak, so easily tired, if his capacity for wonder not so limited, he would abandon forever such fantasies of the supernal. He would learn to perceive in water, leaves and silence more than sufficient of the absolute and marvelous, more than enough to console him for the loss of the ancient dream.

—EDWARD ABBEY, *DESERT SOLITAIRE*

It seemed to me that something extraordinary in the forest was very close to where I stood, moving to the surface and discovery.

—EDWARD O. WILSON, *BIOPHILIA*

If a child is to keep alive his inborn sense of wonder, he needs the companionship of at least one adult who can share it, rediscovering the joy, excitement and mystery of the world we live in.

—RACHEL CARSON, *THE EDGE OF THE SEA*

What happened, what we think happened in distant memory, is built around a small collection of dominating images. In one of my own from the age of seven, I stand in the shallows of Paradise Beach, staring down at a huge jellyfish in water so still and clear that its every detail is revealed as though it were trapped in glass.

—EDWARD O. WILSON, *NATURALIST*

Go and catch a falling star,
   Get with child a mandrake root,
Tell me where all past years are,
   Or who cleft the Devil's foot,
Teach me to hear mermaids
   singing,
Or to keep off envy's stinging,
And find
   What wind
Serves to advance an honest
   mind.
—JOHN DONNE, "SONG"

If the doors of perception were cleansed, we would see
everything as it truly is, infinite.
—WILLIAM BLAKE, ESSAYS

The wilderness has a mysterious tongue
Which teaches awful doubt, or faith so mild,
So solemn, so serene, that man may be,
But for such faith, with nature reconciled . . .

—PERCY BYSSHE SHELLEY, "MONT BLANC"

It began in mystery, and it will end in mystery, but what a savage and beautiful country lies between.

—DIANE ACKERMAN, *A NATURAL HISTORY OF THE SENSES*

In fact, if there is any lesson I have learned in my years of following science, it is that nothing is as it seems. Instead, things are as they seem *plus* the details you are just beginning to notice. New truths rarely overturn old ones; they simply add nuanced brushstrokes to the portrait.

—NATALIE ANGIER, *THE BEAUTY OF THE BEASTLY*

Thus, remarkably, we do not know the true number of species on earth even to the nearest order of magnitude.

—EDWARD O. WILSON, IN *CONSERVATION FOR THE 21ST CENTURY*, EDITED BY DAVID WESTERN AND MARY PEARL

All men by nature desire to know . . . Since we are seeking knowledge, we must inquire of what kind are the causes and the principles, the knowledge of which is Wisdom.

—ARISTOTLE, "METAPHYSICS"

To see a World in a Grain of Sand
  And a Heaven in a Wild Flower,
Hold Infinity in the palm of your hand
  And Eternity in an hour.

—WILLIAM BLAKE, "AUGURIES OF INNOCENCE"

What hidden meaning in this riddle lies?

—JOHANN WOLFGANG VON GOETHE, *FAUST*

The universe is wider than our views of it.

—HENRY DAVID THOREAU, *WALDEN*

Over the past 12 years I have learned that a tree needs space to grow, that coyotes sing down by the creek in January, that I can drive a nail into oak only when it is green, that bees know more about making honey than I do, that love can become sadness, and that there are more questions than answers.

—SUE HUBBELL, *A COUNTRY YEAR*

I ran out in excitement and sure enough here was another aurora [northern light]—a glowing silver bow spanning the Muir Inlet in a magnificent arch right under the zenith. And though colorless and steadfast, its intense, solid, white splendor, noble proportions and fineness of finish excited boundless admiration. In form and proportion it was like a rainbow, a bridge of one span five miles wide, so fine and solid and homogenous in every part, I fancy that if all the stars were raked together into one windrow, fused and welded and run through some celestial rolling mill, all would be required to make this one glowing white colossal bridge . . . Losing all thought of sleep, I ran back to my cabin, carried out blankets and lay down on the ground to keep watch until daybreak, that none of the sky wonders of the glorious night within reach of my eyes might be lost.

—JOHN MUIR, *TRAVELS IN ALASKA*

Science contributes moral as well as material blessings to the world. Its great moral contribution is objectivity, or the scientific point of view. This means doubting everything except facts.

—ALDO LEOPOLD, "SONG OF THE GAVILAN"

We must be true inside, true to ourselves, before we can know a truth that is outside us.

—THOMAS MERTON, "SINCERITY"

One goes to Nature only for hints and half truths. Her facts are crude until you have absorbed or translated them.

—JOHN BURROUGHS, *SIGNS AND SEASONS*

If we can somehow retain places where we can always sense the mystery of the unknown, our lives will be richer.

—SIGURD F. OLSON, "MYSTERY AND THE UNKNOWN"

We come from the land, the sky, from love and the body. From matter and creation. We are, life is, an equation we cannot form or shape, a mystery we can't trace in spite of our attempts to follow it back to its origin, to find out when life began, even in all our stories of when the universe came into being, how the first people emerged. It is a failure of human intelligence and compassion that doesn't wonder about, and love, the mystery of our lives and all the rest.

—LINDA HOGAN, "CREATION"

If we do discover a complete theory, it should in time be understandable in broad principle by everyone, not just a few scientists. Then we shall all, philosophers, scientists, and just ordinary people, be able to take part in the discussion of the question of why it is that we and the universe exist.

—STEPHEN HAWKING, *A BRIEF HISTORY OF TIME*

The moon came up behind the black trees to the east, and the wilderness stood forth, vast, mysterious, still. All at once the silence and the solitude were touched by wild music, thin as air, the faraway gabbling of geese flying at night.

—MARTHA REBEN, *A SHARING OF JOY*

To trace the history of a river, or a raindrop, as John Muir would have done, is also to trace the history of the soul, the history of the mind descending and arising in the body. In both, we constantly seek and stumble on divinity, which, like the cornice feeding the lake and the spring becoming a waterfall, feeds, spills, falls and feeds itself over and over again.

—GRETEL ERHLICH, "RIVER HISTORY"

As the geometer his mind applies
To square the circle, nor for all his wit
Finds the right formula, however he tries,
So strive I with that wonder—how to fit
The image to the sphere; so sought to see
How it maintained the point of rest in it.

—DANTE, *PARADISE*, CANTO XXXIII

Community

Nature writing is not about nature. It is about community.

—Barry Lopez, *The Bloomsbury Review*, September 1998

The power of the community as an organizing principle of nature first became clear to me seventeen years
ago in Mexico, while exploring a tropical forest near the
Mayan ruins of Coba. Canopy after canopy, the dense
woodland rose on trunks and branches, buttresses and
columns, vines and creepers, dangling stems and feeding roots, ferns and flowers and frenzied butterfly wings
toward the morning sky. Rubber trees and strangler figs,
banana trees and giant ferns, cabbage palms and co-
conut palms. Grand old patriarchs and insolent young
upstarts. Healthy trees in the midst of maturity and
disease-ridden invalids half-collapsed into the branches
of charitable neighbors. Looming behemoths with
enough wood in them to build a good-sized country
church and fragile seedlings the size of a candelabrum,
male trees and female trees, withered bachelors and
venerable matriarchs, the whole aswarm with struggle
and color, darkness and radiance, silence and noise,
whistles and hums, barks and chatters, fertility and decay, an ancient green civilization, if you will, in which I

stood gazing upward, like a distant descendent returning to the ancestral manor of his family.

Several days later, snorkeling on the nearby coral
reef at Akumal, I saw even more clearly how fundamental this theme is to nature. Everywhere I looked I saw
not individual organisms in solitary pursuit of basic
needs but an immense and complex society working together cooperatively for the mutual benefit of each
member. Alone in the open sea these often delicate organisms would not last twenty-four hours, but together
they had formed a massive structure that could survive
hurricanes. Everywhere there were vivid examples of
life supporting life. Stinging anemones attached themselves to the shells of hermit crabs, providing a defen-
sive array of poison tentacles in exchange for a regular
supply of food. Shrimp removed parasites—food for the
shrimp—from large fish. The smallest fish gathered together in enormous schools so as to confuse predators.
Coral crevices and caves provided shelter for a rich

spectrum of fauna, much in the way of urban apartment buildings.

Communities, whether natural or human, are one of the organizing principles of the world. Now communities of people are banding together to help protect the communities of the natural world. The Nature Conservancy is now harnessing the power of these people to help protect their surrounding landscapes. Across the country and internationally, local people are beginning to chart the course of their communities' futures, and, at the same time, to implement important conservation measures to protect our wild natural communities.

No man is an *Iland,* intire of it selfe; every man is a peece of the *Continent,* a part of the *maine;* if a *Clod* bee washed away by the Sea, *Europe* is the lesse, as well as if a *Promontorie* were, as well as if a *Mannor* of thy *friends* or of *thine owne* were; any man's *death* diminishes *me,* because I am involved in *Mankinde;* And therefore never send to know for whom the *bell* tolls; It tolls for *thee.*

—JOHN DONNE, MEDITATION XVII

There are no islands anymore.

—EDNA ST. VINCENT MILLAY, TITLE OF POEM WRITTEN IN 1940

One touch of nature makes the whole world kin.

—WILLIAM SHAKESPEARE, *TROILUS AND CRESSIDA*

Snowflakes, leaves, humans, plants, raindrops, stars, molecules, microscopic entities all come in communities. The singular cannot in Reality exist.

—PAULA GUNN ALLEN, *GRANDMOTHERS OF THE LIGHT*

On some summer vacation or some country weekend we realize that what we are experiencing is more than merely a relief from the pressures of city life; that we have not merely escaped *from* something but also into something; that we have joined the greatest of all communities, which is not that of men alone but of everything that shares with us the great adventure of being alive.

—JOSEPH WOOD KRUTCH, "MAN'S ANCIENT, POWERFUL LINK TO NATURE"

Shall I not have intelligence with the earth? Am I not partly leaves and vegetable mould myself?

—HENRY DAVID THOREAU, *WALDEN*

Conservation is sometimes perceived as stopping everything cold, as holding whooping cranes in higher esteem than people. It is up to science to spread the understanding that the choice is not between wild places or people, it is between a rich or an impoverished existence for Man.

—THOMAS E. LOVEJOY, QUOTED IN *BALANCING ON THE BRINK OF EXTINCTION* EDITED BY KATHRYN A. KOHM

———•••———

Whether the universe is atoms or a system, let this first be established: I am a part of the whole which is governed by nature.

—MARCUS AURELIUS, *MEDITATIONS*

It is not bigness that should be our goal. We must attempt, rather, to bring people back to . . . the warmth of community, to the worth of individual effort and responsibility . . . and of individuals working together as a community, to better their lives and their children's future.

—ROBERT F. KENNEDY, IN HIS 1966 SPEECH
"REBUILDING A SENSE OF COMMUNITY"

Why should I feel lonely? Is not our planet in the Milky Way?

—HENRY DAVID THOREAU, *WALDEN*

As soon as we take one thing by itself, we find it hitched to everything in the universe.

—JOHN MUIR, *JOURNALS*

When you make a world tolerable for yourself you make a world tolerable for others.

—ANAÏS NIN, *THE DIARY OF ANAÏS NIN*

Rain does not fall on one roof alone.

—CAMEROON PROVERB

All ethics so far evolved rest upon a single premise: that the individual is a member of a community of interdependent parts. His instincts prompt him to compete for his place in the community, but his ethics prompt him also to co-operate (perhaps in order that there may be a place to compete for). The land ethic simply enlarges the boundaries of the community to include soils, waters, plants, and animals, or, collectively, the land.

—ALDO LEOPOLD, "THE LAND ETHIC"

We abuse land because we regard it as a commodity belonging to us. When we see land as a community to which we belong, we may begin to use it with love and respect.

—ALDO LEOPOLD, *A SAND COUNTY ALMANAC*

Conservation means harmony between men and land. When land does well for its owner, and the owner does well by his land; when both end up better, by reason of their partnerships, we have conservation.

—ALDO LEOPOLD, *ROUND RIVER*

No individual is isolated. He who is sad, saddens others.

—ANTOINE DE SAINT-EXUPÉRY, "FLIGHT TO ARRAS"

Gradually I am becoming a part of the community.

—PIONEERING ANTHROPOLOGIST MARGARET MEAD, DESCRIBING
HER STAY ON SAMOA IN 1925 (FROM *LETTERS FROM THE FIELD*)

Our relationships with wild animals were once contrac-
tual—principled agreements, established and maintained
in a spirit of reciprocity and mythic in their pervasive-
ness. Among hunting peoples in general in the northern
hemisphere, these agreements derived from a sense of
mutual obligation and courtesy.

—BARRY LOPEZ, "RENEGOTIATING THE CONTRACTS"

If we all treated others as we wish to be treated ourselves, then decency and stability would have to prevail.
I suggest that we execute such a pact with our planet.

—STEPHEN JAY GOULD, *NATURAL HISTORY* MAGAZINE

To restore the land one must live and work in a place. To work in a place is to work with others. People who work together in a place become a community, and a community, in time, grows a culture. To work on behalf of the wild is to restore culture.

—GARY SNYDER, "REDISCOVERY OF TURTLE ISLAND"

I feel this communion, this strange attunement, most readily with large white pines, a little less with big spruces, sugar maples, beeches, or oaks. Clearly white pines and I are on the same wavelength. What I give back to the trees I cannot imagine. I hope they receive something, because trees are among my closest friends.

—ANNE LABASTILLE, *WOODSWOMAN*

Do not dishonour the earth lest you dishonour the
    spirit of man.

    —HENRY BESTON, *THE OUTERMOST HOUSE*

Never doubt that a small group of thoughtful, committed citizens can change the world. Indeed, it's the only
thing that ever has.

    —MARGARET MEAD, *CULTURE AND COMMITMENT*

Grief can take care of itself, but to get the full value of a
joy you must have somebody to divide it with.

    —MARK TWAIN, *AUTOBIOGRAPHY*

Man is whole when he is in tune with the wind, the stars and the hills as well as with his neighbors. Being in tune with the apartment or the community is part of the secret, being in tune with the universe is the entire secret.

—WILLIAM O. DOUGLAS, *My Wilderness*

When we run out of country, we will run out of stories. When we run out of stories, we will run out of sanity. We will not be able to depend on each other for anything—not for friendship or mercy, and certainly not for love or understanding.

—RICK BASS, "ON WILLOW CREEK"

Our lack of intimacy with each other is in direct proportion to our lack of intimacy with the land. We have taken our love inside and abandoned the wild.

—TERRY TEMPEST WILLIAMS, "WINTER SOLSTICE AT THE MOAB SLOUGH"

One revived rural community could be the beginning of the renewal of our country. But to be authentic, this would have to be a revival accomplished mainly by the community itself. Done by the ancient rule of neighborliness, by the love of precious things, and by the wish to be at home.

—WENDELL BERRY

Love the animals, love the plants, love everything. If you love everything, you will perceive the divine mystery in things. Once you perceive it, you will begin to comprehend it better every day. And you will come at last to love the whole world with an all-embracing love.

—FYODOR DOSTOYEVSKY, *THE BROTHERS KARAMAZOV*

It is from numberless diverse acts of courage and belief that human history is shaped. Each time a man stands up for an ideal, or acts to improve the lot of others, or strikes out against injustice, he sends forth a tiny ripple of hope; and crossing each other from a million different centers of energy and daring, those ripples build a current which can sweep down the mightiest walls of oppression and resistance.

—ROBERT F. KENNEDY, IN HIS "DAY OF AFFIRMATION" SPEECH AT THE UNIVERSITY OF CAPE TOWN, SOUTH AFRICA, 1966

Stewardship

Something will have gone out of us as a people if we ever let the remaining wilderness be destroyed . . . We need wilderness preserved . . . because it was the challenge against which our character as a people was formed.

—WALLACE STEGNER,
"WILDERNESS AND THE GEOGRAPHY OF HOPE"

The Americans who poured through the Cumberland Gap, who homesteaded the Kansas prairie, who filled to overflowing the Arcady of California, carried with them an Old World sense of stewardship, and of land as property to be acquired and defended. In the early 20th century, as the last vestiges of the western frontier began to vanish from the maps, a new mode of thinking about the landscape arose. Thinkers such as Bob Marshall and Aldo Leopold proposed that the bold new conservation tradition started in Yellowstone National Park (1872) be greatly expanded to include permanent protection for wilderness areas in the national forests. In this way, large roadless tracts without any form of commercial development could be preserved. As a result of their efforts, the world's first wilderness area, the Gila in New Mexico, was designated in 1924.

Today we work to preserve nature for many reasons. Nature has practical value to us, as a source of food, water, recreation, building materials, minerals, and pharmaceuticals. For me, the most powerful reasons have always been the ethical and aesthetic—that we would not be complete human beings without the beauty of nature surrounding and enriching our lives.

In today's world, many species and natural communities need a helping hand to survive. In many cases, this requires not just preserving habitat for them but also taking care of it.

Stewardship, or the management of lands and waters for conservation purposes, is how The Nature Conservancy ultimately achieves its goal of long-term protection of biodiversity. The organization's stewardship staff manages more than 1,340 nature preserves throughout the United States.

It is not just professional stewards who take care of the land. Thousands of dedicated volunteers of all ages, from schoolchildren to retired men and women, devote their time and talents to helping the Conservancy achieve its mission every day. Conservancy volunteers perform tasks as far ranging as clearing brush to counting birds to answering the phones.

One does not have to be affiliated with any particular organization, however, to be a steward. Stewards are caretakers and protectors. They seek to understand our natural world and provide for its long-term existence. Stewardship, then, is a job for everyone, challenging all of us to act as advocates for the protection of species and ecosystems.

In the end, our society will be defined not only by what we create but by what we refuse to destroy.

—JOHN C. SAWHILL,
PRESIDENT AND CEO OF THE NATURE CONSERVANCY

When my son runs down the hill through the trees, shouting for mama and laughing as freely as only a baby can laugh, I cup my hands in stubborn hopefulness, making to him the promise my mama could never keep to me. I will make this place safe for him, bring him back to this landscape throughout his life, this wild country of beauty and hope and mystery.

—DOROTHY ALLISON, "PROMISES"

In the end, we conserve only what we love. We will love only what we understand. We will understand only what we are taught.

—BABA DIUOM, SENEGALESE POET

Friends at home! I charge you to spare, preserve and cherish some portion of your primitive forests; for when these are cut away I apprehend they will not be easily replaced.

—HORACE GREELEY, *NEW YORK TRIBUNE,* 1851

The Lakota loved the earth and all things of the earth, the attachment growing with age. The old people came literally to love the soil and they sat or reclined on the ground with a feeling of being close to a mothering power. It was good for the skin to touch the earth and the old people liked to remove their moccasins and walk with bare feet on the sacred earth . . . The Lakota knew that lack of respect for growing, living things soon leads to a lack of respect for humans too.

—CHIEF STANDING BEAR, *LAKOTA*

In losing stewardship we lose fellowship; we become outcasts from the great neighborhood of creation.

—WENDELL BERRY, *THE GIFT OF GOOD LAND*

We must preserve our sacred places in order to know our place in time, our reach to eternity.

—N. SCOTT MOMADAY, *THE MAN MADE OF WORDS*

Let man heal the hurt places and revere whatever is still miraculously pristine.

—DAVID R. BROWER, IN ELIOT PORTER'S
SUMMER ISLAND: PENOBSCOT COUNTRY

No other nation on Earth so swiftly wasted its birthright; no other, in time, made such an effort to save what was left.

—WALLACE STEGNER, *THE SOUND OF MOUNTAIN WATER*

Our government is like a rich and foolish spendthrift who has inherited a magnificent estate in perfect order, and then has left his fields and meadows, forests and parks to be sold and plundered and wasted.

—JOHN MUIR, "THE AMERICAN FORESTS"

I am quite seriously proposing that we give legal rights to forests, oceans, rivers, and other so-called "natural objects" in the environment—indeed, to the natural environment as a whole.

—CHRISTOPHER D. STONE, "SHOULD TREES HAVE STANDING?"

All civilized governments are now realizing that it is their duty . . . to preserve, unharmed, tracts of wild nature, with thereon the wild things the destruction of which means the destruction of half the charm of wild nature . . .

—THEODORE ROOSEVELT, *AFRICAN GAME TRAILS*

A thing is right when it tends to preserve the integrity, stability, and beauty of the biotic community. It is wrong when it tends otherwise.

—ALDO LEOPOLD, "THE CONSERVATION ETHIC"

We are the fire which burns the country.

—BANTU PROVERB

A continent ages quickly once we come. The natives live in harmony with it. But the foreigner destroys, cuts down the trees, drains the water so that in a short time the soil starts to blow away as it has blown in every old country . . . The earth gets tired of being exploited. A country was made to be as we found it.

—ERNEST HEMINGWAY, *THE GREEN HILLS OF AFRICA*

———

Conservation can be defined as the wise use of our natural environment: it is, in the final analysis, the highest form of national thrift—the prevention of waste and despoilment while preserving, improving and renewing the quality and usefulness of all our resources.

—PRESIDENT JOHN F. KENNEDY

We stand now where two roads diverge. But unlike the roads in Robert Frost's familiar poem, they are not equally fair. The road we have long been traveling is deceptively easy, a smooth superhighway on which we progress with great speed, but at its end lies disaster. The other fork of the road—the one "less traveled by"— offers our last, our only chance to reach a destination that assures the preservation of our earth.

—RACHEL CARSON, *SILENT SPRING*

Man is born to die. His works are short-lived. Buildings crumble. Monuments decay, wealth vanish, but Katahdin in all its glory forever shall remain the mountain of the people of Maine.

—FORMER MAINE GOVERNOR PERCIVAL B. BAXTER,
IN PRESENTING THE FINAL TRACT OF BAXTER STATE PARK
TO THE PEOPLE OF MAINE, 1962

Each generation has its own rendezvous with the land, for despite fee titles and claims of ownership, we are all brief tenants on this planet. By choice, or by default, we will carve out a land legacy for our heirs. We can misuse the land and diminish the usefulness of resources, or we can create a world in which physical affluence and affluence of the spirit go hand in hand. History tells us that earlier civilizations have declined because they did not learn to live in harmony with the land.

—STEWART LEE UDALL, *THE QUIET CRISIS*

———

One of the great dreams of man must be to find some place between the extremes of nature and civilization where it is possible to live without regret.

—BARRY LOPEZ, "SEARCHING FOR ANCESTORS"

The enterprise of conservation is a revolution, an evolution of the spirit. We call to the land—and the land calls back.

—TERRY TEMPEST WILLIAMS, "YELLOWSTONE"

As I watched the woods and listened to the talk of old trappers, I saw that it was best to leave a little seed in the country, and to trap according to the scarcity and abundance of the fur sign.

—JOHN HAINES, THE STARS, THE SNOW, THE FIRE

The land was ours before we were the land's.

—ROBERT FROST, "THE GIFT"

We Africans have treated certain birds, animals and plants with the highest regard. In the cultural beliefs of some communities, the very existence of their lineage may depend upon a given species . . . [This] is a moral principle whose observance has preserved Africa's wildlife heritage for generations. The future of living things is largely affected by the ethics of those who have influence over them.

—PEREZ OLINDO, *ELEPHANTS: THE DECIDING DECADE*

If mountain gorillas are to survive and propagate, far more active conservation measures urgently need to be undertaken. The question remains, is it already too late?

—DIAN FOSSEY, *GORILLAS IN THE MIST*

Alive the grizzly is a symbol of freedom and understanding—a sign that man can learn to conserve what is left of the earth. Extinct, it will be another fading testimony to things man should have learned about but was too preoccupied with himself to notice. In its beleaguered condition, it is above all a symbol of what man is doing to the entire planet. If we can learn from these experiences, and learn rationally, both the grizzly and man may have a chance to survive.

—FRANK C. CRAIGHEAD, *TRACK OF THE GRIZZLY*

A key question is that of our ethical obligations to the nonhuman world. The very notion rattles the foundations of occidental thought. Native American religious beliefs, although not identical coast to coast, are overwhelmingly in support of a full and sensitive acknowledgement of the subjecthood—the intrinsic value—of nature.

—GARY SNYDER, "THE REDISCOVERY OF TURTLE ISLAND"

The land belongs to the future . . . We come and go but the land is always here. And the people who love it and understand it are the people who own it—for a little while.

—WILLA CATHER, *O PIONEERS!*

It is good to realize that, if love and peace can prevail on earth, and if we can teach our children to honor nature's gifts, the joys and beauties of the outdoors will be here forever.

—PRESIDENT JIMMY CARTER, *AN OUTDOOR JOURNAL*

Natural philosophy has brought into clear relief the following paradox of human existence. The drive toward perpetual expansion—or personal freedom—is basic to the human spirit. But to sustain it we need the most delicate, knowing steward-ship of the living world that can be devised. Expansion and stewardship may appear at first to be conflicting goals, but they are not. The depth of the conservation ethic will be measured by the extent to which each of the two approaches to nature is used to reshape and reinforce the other. The paradox can be resolved by changing its premises into forms more suited to ultimate survival, by which I mean protection of the human spirit.

—EDWARD O. WILSON, *BIOPHILIA*

It is our task in our time and in our generation to hand down undiminished to those who come after us, as was handed down to us by those who went before, the natural wealth and beauty which is ours.

—PRESIDENT JOHN F. KENNEDY

Selected Biographies

Edward Abbey authored over twenty books, including the novel *The Brave Cowboy,* which was made into the film *Lonely Are the Brave,* starring Kirk Douglas, and the ever-popular *Desert Solitaire,* a memoir of his years of working in Arches National Park.

Ansel Adams was to American photography in the 20th century what such pioneers as Timothy O'Sullivan and William Henry Jackson were to the same art form in the 19th century. His stature, like theirs, grows with every passing year.

Aristotle studied under Plato at the Academy in Athens from 367 to 347 B.C. He later was hired by Philip of Macedon to teach his rebellious teenage son, who grew up to become Alexander the Great. One of the great thinkers of history, Aristotle enjoyed immense popularity during the Renaissance, when modern Western civilization was forming.

Marcus Aurelius served as emperor of Rome from 161 to 180 A.D. He is one of the most eminent Stoic philosophers and is the author of *Meditations,* written in Greek and the single most important Roman Stoic document.

Mary Austin was the author of *The Land of Little Rain* (1903), a collection of essays on the desert and foothill country between Death Valley and the High Sierra.

Rick Bass is one of his generation's passionate defenders of wilderness. His books include *The Deer Pasture* (1985), *Winter* (1990), *The Nine-Mile Wolves* (1994), and *The New Wolves* (1998). He lives in Montana.

George Caitlin traveled west into the wild Missouri River country in the 1830s, after the Age of Trapping but before the first wave of homesteaders arrived. His paintings documented such tribes as the Mandan in North Dakota, which would soon disappear.

Albert Camus, the author of such influential works as *The Stranger* and *The Plague,* was awarded the Nobel Prize for literature in 1963. He died in a car crash in the south of France several months later, at the age of forty-three.

Sally Carrighar's many nature books include *One Day at Teton Marsh* (1944) and *One Day on Beetle Rock* (1947).

Rachel Carson, a research biologist by profession, authored such influential books as *Under the Sea Wind* (1941), *The Sea Around Us* (1950), and *Silent Spring* (1962).

Willa Cather wrote of her childhood on the Nebraska prairie and of her later life in the Southwest in such classic novels as *O Pioneers!* (1913) and *The Professor's House* (1925).

Frank C. Craighead, together with his brother John Craighead, literally created the science of grizzly bear ecology. Both brothers worked through the 1950s and 1960s in Yellowstone National Park. Frank is the author of *Track of the Grizzly* (1979).

Charles Darwin will forever be known as the author of *The Origin of Species* (1859), the work that revolutionized human thinking on the subjects of evolution and natural selection.

Jan DeBlieu lives on the Outer Banks of North Carolina. She is the author of such noted works as *Hatteras Journal* (1989) and, more recently, *Wind* (1998), which was awarded the Burroughs Medal for nature writing.

Annie Dillard was awarded the Pulitzer Prize for nonfiction in 1975 for her book *Pilgrim at Tinker Creek.* Since then she has taught at Wesleyan University at Middleton, Connecticut, and produced several more distinguished works of nonfiction and fiction.

Isak Dinesen moved to Africa from her native Denmark as a young woman, and lived for a number of years on a coffee plantation just outside Nairobi. When Hemingway received the Nobel Prize in 1954, he said he did not deserve it so long as Isak Dinesen had not received it for her book *Out of Africa* (1939).

Marjory Stoneman Douglas will forever be associated with her beloved Florida Everglades. Long before it was fashionable, Douglas was fighting for the swamp fauna and flora of south Florida in such books as *The Everglades* (1947).

William O. Douglas served as an Associate Justice of the U.S. Supreme Court and was known as a fierce defender of the Bill of Rights and the environment. Among his many books is the classic *My Wilderness* (1960), which describes his many favorite places in North America.

Ralph Waldo Emerson was one of the leading exponents of Transcendentalism in 19th-century American literature.

Louise Erdrich is one of the country's most accomplished Native American writers. Her books include both works of fiction and nonfiction, most recently *The Antelope Wife* (1997).

Gretel Erhlich's book *The Solace of Open Spaces* (1985) was published to immediate acclaim. Although for many years she lived in northern Wyoming, she has more recently called the California coast near Santa Barbara home.

Colin Fletcher hiked a 200-mile segment of the Grand Canyon in 1967. His book *The Man Who Walked*

Through Time (1968) is now considered one of the classics of exploration literature.

Dian Fossey, an associate of anthropologist Louis Leakey, worked for many years on behalf of the upland gorillas of the African highlands. Her memoir *Gorillas in the Mist* (1985) was later made into a film with Sigourney Weaver in the role of the naturalist.

Robert Frost owns the distinction of being the only American poet to ever win the Pulitzer Prize four times. Although Frost never received the Nobel Prize, he did enjoy other honors, including a reading at the presidential inauguration of fellow New Englander John F. Kennedy.

Jane Goodall worked for many years with the chimpanzees of the Gombe Sanctuary in Tanzania. She has worked tirelessly on their behalf as a lecturer and public spokesperson.

John Haines, the former poet laureate of Alaska, is the author of such celebrated works of literature as *The*

Owl in the Mask of Dreamer (1994) and *The Stars, The Snow, The Fire* (1987).

Jim Harrison is best known for his novella *Legends of the Fall* (1980), which was subsequently made into a film that garnered an Oscar for best cinematography. Several of his other stories have been made into films, including *Wolf* (1984), which later served as the basis for the film by the same name starring Jack Nicholson.

Heracleitus, who lived from 540 to 480 B.C., is the grandfather of Western philosophy. No other early thinker had as much influence on Socrates and his student, Plato.

Linda Hogan is an English professor at the University of Colorado. She is the author of such popular novels as *Mean Spirit* (1990), which was a finalist for the Pulitzer Prize, *Solar Storms* (1994), and *Power* (1998).

John Keats, the greatest poet of the Romantic period, died in 1821 at the age of twenty-six. Scholars have often compared his talent to that of Shakespeare. We will never know what this literary giant (who stood five feet one inch tall) might have accomplished had tuberculosis not struck him down just as he was beginning to dazzle the world.

Clare Leighton was the author of *Southern Harvest* (1942), a collection of essays on country life in the Old South.

Aldo Leopold will forever be associated with his seminal works of nature philosophy, most notably *The Sand County Almanac* (1949), which postulated what is now known as the land ethic.

Barry Lopez has been hailed as a "master nature writer" by *The New York Times Book Review*. His books include *Of Wolves and Men* (1976), *Arctic Dreams* (1986), which won a National Book Award, and most recently *About This Life* (1999).

Robert Marshall, together with his contemporary Aldo Leopold, helped to shape modern thinking on the role of wilderness in civilization. The immense Bob Marshall Wilderness Area in northern Montana is named for this influential environmental leader.

Peter Matthiessen is one of the finest contemporary American writers of prose. Among his many works of fiction and nonfiction is *The Snow Leopard* (1968).

N. Scott Momaday is the author of the Pulitzer Prize–winning *The Way to Rainy Mountain* (1978). A professor of English and American literature at the University of New Mexico, Albuquerque, he now divides his time between writing and painting.

John Muir devoted his life to the celebration and preservation of nature, especially that of his beloved Range of Light (the Sierra Nevadas) in California. No other author since Thoreau has had such an impact on the relationship between American civilization and nature.

Richard Nelson received the Burroughs Medal for nature writing in 1990 for his memoir of life in southeast Alaska, *The Island Within*. Nelson is also known for his numerous works of cultural anthropology.

Georgia O'Keeffe is one of America's greatest artists. After living many years in the East with her husband,

Alfred Stieglitz, the New York photographer and gallery owner, O'Keeffe eventually moved to northern New Mexico, where she lived until her death at the age of ninety-nine.

Sigurd F. Olson will forever be associated with the Minnesota lake country. Among his many popular works are such classics as *Runes of the North* and *Reflections from the North Country.*

Plato was a disciple of Socrates and a teacher of Aristotle. He lived from 428 to 348 or 347 B.C. His works, which take the form of dialogues with his master, Socrates, include *The Republic, Laws, Phaedrus, Symposium, Timaeus, Phaedo,* and *Apology.* These books, which would have been lost during the Dark Ages but for the Arabs (who saved them), form the textual basis for modern Western philosophy.

Marjorie Kinnan Rawlings was the author of *The Yearling* (1938), which was awarded the Pulitzer Prize in 1938, and *Cross Creek* (1942). Her writings concerned life in rural Florida before it was so dramatically transformed by growth and development.

Noh J. Raymur, the Scottish poet laureate, was awarded the Royal Medal in 1915 for his epic poem "The Argolid." He spent most of his life in a country cottage near Blair Castle.

William Shakespeare was born on April 23, 1564, and died on the same day in 1616. No other author in the English language has been so influential. His plays continue to enjoy immense popularity, both on stage and in film adaptation.

Wallace Stegner taught for many years in the writing program at Stanford University. His many books include such classics as *The Sound of Mountain Water* (1951) and *Angle of Repose* (1967), the latter of which was awarded the Pulitzer Prize for fiction.

Henry David Thoreau spent most of his life in and around eastern Massachusetts. A graduate of Harvard, his books and essays include *Walden,* "Civil Disobedience," "Walking," and "On John Brown's Body."

Walt Whitman, together with Emily Dickinson, helped to form the basis for modern American poetry. No other American poet has had so many elementary and high schools named for him. Part of this honor was bestowed upon Whitman for his wonderful poetry, and part of it came on behalf of a grateful nation for his tireless charity work in the military hospitals of the Civil War.

Terry Tempest Williams, who lives in Castle Valley near Moab, Utah, is the author of such well-known works as *Pieces of White Shell* (1984), *Refuge* (1991), and *Coyote's Canyon* (1989).

Edward O. Wilson has twice been awarded the Pulitzer Prize for nonfiction. Formerly an entomology professor at Harvard University, Wilson is now retired and spends much of his time speaking out on behalf of biodiversity.

William Wordsworth is known primarily for his "Preface to the Lyrical Ballads," an essay he cowrote with Samuel Taylor Coleridge, which revolutionized English poetry, and his autobiographical poem *The Prelude*. In later years he became poet laureate and exercised considerable influence on younger poets such as Tennyson.

William Butler Yeats, the Irish lyric poet and dramatist, received the Nobel Prize in 1923. He was also active in Irish politics and served as one of the first senators of the Irish Free State in the 1920s.

Index

A

Abbey, Edward, 26, 30, 86, 89, 141, 158
Ackerman, Diane, 121, 161
Adams, Ansel, 94, 151
Alcmaeon, 156
Allen, Paula Gunn, 175
Allison, Dorothy, 20, 192
Anderson, Lorraine, 20
Angier, Natalie, 98, 105, 161
Aristotle, 103, 162
Aurelius, Marcus, 88, 176
Austin, Mary, 86

B

Babbitt, Bruce, 53
Bacon, Francis, 50, 73
Balboa, Vasco Nuñez de, 62
Banks, Sir Joseph, 58

Bass, Rick, 38, 103, 120, 122, 149, 183
Baxter, Percival B., 198
Benét, Stephen Vincent, 19
Berry, Wendell, 113, 184, 194
Beston, Henry, 32, 182
Bishop, Elizabeth, 78
Blake, William, 140, 160, 162
Bly, Carol, 13
Brooks, Paul, 16
Brower, David R., 194
Bruce, James, 59
Burroughs, John, 31, 114, 120, 165
Byron, Lord, 31, 116

C

Campbell, David, 63
Camus, Albert, 32
Carrighar, Sally, 107

Wells, H. G., 82
Whitman, Walt, 99, 113, 136
Whittier, John Greenleaf, 148
Wilde, Oscar, 101
Williams, Terry Tempest, 16, 39,
   113, 124, 183, 200
Wilson, Edward O. 30, 46, 158,
   159, 162, 204

Wordsworth, Dorothy, 135
Wordsworth, William, 17, 101,
   134

Y

Yeats, William Butler, 28, 142